GREaT

IDEAS
FOR TEACHERS

by Bev Gundersen

illustrated by Roberta K. Loman

STANDARD PUBLISHING
Cincinnati, Ohio   14-03062

This book is lovingly dedicated to
Signe and Mandy
who taught me to wisely use
all that God has entrusted to me.

"From everyone who has been given much, much will
be demanded; and from the one who has been entrusted
with much, much more will be asked" (Luke 12:48).

All Scripture quotations in this publication are from the Holy
Bible, New International Version. Copyright © 1973, 1978,
1984, International Bible Society. Used by permission of
Zondervan Bible Publishers.

Library of Congress Cataloging-in-Publication Data

Gundersen, Bev.
    Great ideas for teachers/by Bev Gundersen.
        p.   cm.
    Includes index.
    ISBN 0-87403-782-4
    1. Teaching—Aids and devices.   I. Title.
LB1044.88.G86   1991   90-49446
371.3'078--dc20   CIP

Bag Books

These bags are made from plastic zipper-bags. Cut poster board pages the same width and 1" shorter than the bags. This makes allowance for the zipper closing. Glue pictures to both sides of each page. Insert the page in the bag with the zipper side at the left. Zip shut. Punch several holes just to the right of each zipper opening. Attach all the pages of the book with metal rings. This will allow you to open the bags and change picture pages as desired.

A busy book version can be made by placing the zipper opening at the top of the page instead of the left side. Activity objects such as puzzles, lacing pictures, matching games, etc. can be placed in these bags.

Banners

classroom banners

You don't have to be able to sew in order to make nice banners. Use burlap or felt for backgrounds. Designs may be copied from reproducible pictures or embroidery patterns directly onto the background using permanent-ink markers, or they can be cut from felt and glued on. When you want to use several colors of felt for a single figure or picture, make two copies of the pattern — one on tracing paper and the other on typing or tissue paper. Cut the plain paper pattern apart and use it to cut the different colors of felt. Allow a tiny overlap on bottom pieces and adjoining areas instead of trying to match edges exactly. Glue the felt pieces on the tracing paper pattern so each segment is in the correct spot. Layer parts so the design has a three dimensional look. Cut out the completed tracing paper picture close to the felt. Glue this entire picture on the burlap. The tracing paper will hold the whole design together and yet will never be seen. Letters can be cut freehand or by using stencils. Lay the stencils upside down on the felt and trace the letters with a fine tip permanent-ink marker. Permanent ink won't smear on hands or felt when you add the glue. Cut just inside the marking to eliminate any ink showing through to the other side.

special occasion banners

Banners are not limited to room decoration. Use them for teaching unit themes or celebrating special occasions. A "Happy Birthday" or "Congratulations!" banner is a special way for a class or family to honor a member's important day.

nature banner

A nature banner with pockets for displaying God's creations is a must for camps, VBS, or even homes. Use sturdy, clear, pliable plastic for it. Make several rows of pockets and sew them to the plastic background. When sewing on plastic, use large stitches so the plastic won't tear. Reinforce the sewing by placing colorful plastic tape over it. The plastic allows you to put even damp items such as pebbles from a stream or field flowers in the pockets. By using transparent plastic each item can easily be seen. You might want to add a caption such as "Praise the Lord" or "He Created All Things." This could be lettered directly onto the plastic with a permanent-ink marker or cut out of felt or paper and glued on. Glue or tack the banner to a sturdy dowel for hanging.

Bible Times Costumes

Bible times costumes add much to the interest and effectiveness of lessons. They are also handy to have for programs. Clothing designs were very plain in that period, so you can make costumes to fit any student very easily.

robe

Robes were shaped much like a loose fitting, long-sleeved T-shirt. An adult robe was ankle length, while a child's was knee length. Cut the robe on a fold at the shoulders. Make it as wide as the measurement of your arms from wrist to wrist. The length should be equal to the distance from the shoulder fold to ankle or knee, depending on whether it is for an adult or child. The main body part of the robe should be loose, allowing sufficient room for your body plus some "moving around" space. Allow 5/8" for seams. Cut a neck hole in the center of the top fold. Because the robe will slip over the head, cut a short slit from the hole opening down the center back. Finish this slit and neck opening with a narrow hem or binding. Sew sleeve and side seams as indicated in the illustration. Finish sleeve openings and bottom of robe with a narrow hem. Use a small piece of velcro or a snap to fasten the neck opening. Fabric colors were often dependent on the materials from which they were woven. The most common material was wool or linen so the cloth was tan, cream, brown, or gray. Women's robes were decorated with embroidery or different colored threads woven into the fabric. The wealthy loved the deep reds and purples of more costly cloth and even wore silk with precious-metal threads woven in it.

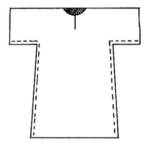

coat

This garment is cut similar to the robe but with shorter body and sleeve lengths. Open this garment all the way down the front in-

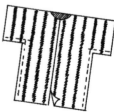

stead of making a back slit. Men's coats often had brown and black stripes that ran from the shoulders to the hem.

mantle

This was a large straight strip of cloth which was draped around the body and usually had one end thrown over the shoulder in back.

belt or girdle

This is just a straight cloth strip of any desired length and width. Be sure it is long enough to go around the waist and either tie or tuck in. Both men and women wore belts to keep robes in place. Women's belts were often striped or decorated in some manner.

head coverings

For men these could be a simple headband tied in back, a cap alone, or a cap with a strip of cloth wrapped around it several times and tucked in place. Shepherds often wore a square cloth over the head which was kept in place with a strip of cloth. Women's head coverings were straight strips of cloth in between the belt and mantle width for size. These veils were long enough to cover the head and face. Ties were not used to keep these veils in place.

sandals

Sandals or bare feet were the order of the day. A sandal can be made by drawing around the foot onto sturdy cardboard. Punch holes as shown and use long shoestrings for laces.

crowns

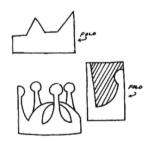

Crowns can be made from lightweight poster board (also called tag board). Glue a long strip of metallic gift wrap to the poster board. Fold this strip in half three times. To make crown 1 draw this pattern and cut it out. Unfold it. Use rhinestones or old jewelry pieces as precious stones. Lap the ends of the crown to fit student's head size and staple them together. For crown 2, use the second pattern. It is made in the same way as crown 1 but with an added step. Bend the tall pieces to the center and paste them together. Crowns also make good rewards to students for attendance, memorization, or bringing visitors.

masks

Masks can add real personality to Bible characters. By adding facial features and hair or beards you can vary a basic pattern.

poster board mask

Draw and cut out the face shape from poster board. Cut out eye holes. Draw a mouth or add a 3-dimensional one. To add a mouth, draw and cut out a piece from construction paper. Cut a slit in the face shape and push the mouth piece into it. Draw and cut out the hair and nose from construction paper. Cut along the slashes and curl these strips with your scissors. Glue the hair onto the mask forehead. Curl the nose up at the end. A beard can be added in the same manner as the hair.

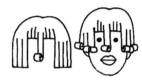

panty hose mask

Bend a wire coat hanger into an oval shape. Cut a leg off panty hose. Stretch this stocking part over the hanger and tie it tightly at both ends. Make facial features by drawing them with permanent-ink markers or gluing on pieces of felt, wiggly eyes, or buttons. Yarn or fake fur makes good hair and beards. Hold the mask in front of your face by the hook end of the hanger.

angel wings

Make these from poster board. Cover them with aluminum foil, metallic gift wrap, or spray them with metallic paint. Punch 3 holes where shown. Use twill tape for tie and insert it through the top holes. Pull the tie over the shoulders and crisscross the ends in front. Draw the tie to the back and insert both ends through the bottom hole. Pull these ends around the waist from back to front and tie.

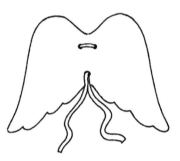

Booklets

Draw or glue pictures and/or stories on each page that tell something about what is being studied. Construction paper makes good pages.

Staple the pages together or punch holes in them and use yarn, shoelaces, etc. to tie them together. This is a good way to review a unit in church school. When the unit is done, the student takes the booklet home. You can do booklets on memory verses, topics, or Bible characters like "This Is Your Life — Apostle Paul."

Bulletin Boards

Bulletin boards add interest and more learning power to any classroom. Although most are made of cork, a lightweight substitute can be made from Styrofoam. Choose the kind that is used in building insulation and cut it into any shape or size desired. Cover the board with burlap and staple it onto the back side of the Styrofoam.

A bulletin board should be the focal point of the room. Be sure to hang it at your students' eye level. Keeping it changed and current is a must. Boards can be used to teach lessons, to stress monthly activities, as a review, to display student work, or to promote thinking. There are many helpful bulletin board books for sale.

Busy Books

Busy books are great for teaching hand-eye coordination, using the sense of touch, and keeping the interest of young children while teaching them about God. Professional pattern manufacturers have several designs on the market but you can also make your own. Use pictures that have large pieces as your patterns. Cut these pieces out of brightly-colored cloth or felt and work out segments that can be used tactily, that is segments that can snap, button, tie, braid, fasten with velcro, be placed in pockets, counted, etc.

If you are concerned about young children putting these removable pieces in their mouths, use attractive buttons and sew them at key places in the picture. Buttons come in all shapes and sizes these days and, although not removable, add a special "feel" to a busy book. Children can count the buttons, decide how many there are of each color, etc.

Buttons

Big, bold, message buttons are good "attention getters" and allow you to present the lesson aim or memory verse in a new way. Cut a large circle from lightweight poster board. Print the message on the "button" and decorate it with markers, stickers, or add-ons, such as sequins, glitter, or silk flowers. Tape a safety pin on the back of the poster board to pin it on.

Chalkboard

Cover sturdy cardboard with Con-Tact blackboard plastic. This product (Rubbermaid Company) comes in rolls like other adhesive-plastic and can be used for doors, dividers, etc. Use regular chalk and facial tissues or paper towels for erasing. Make a small board to stick inside a folding flannelboard for use on outings, at camps, or at VBS. You can make a whiteboard on the other side of the cardboard to provide a portable teaching center for your class. (See WHITEBOARD.)

Character Boards

Use a large piece of heavy poster board or cardboard. Cut out a 9" oval for the head and 4" circles for hands about 6"-10" below the head and about 12" apart. Draw or paint details of the character such as hair, clothing, jewelry, etc. You can score the board and fold it in half to allow extra arm movement. Students insert their heads and arms to become the character. This can be used for words as well as people or animals. Words with "O" such as "joy" or "hope" work especially well. These character boards help young children act out Bible stories. Some basic characters, such as a shepherd, king, woman, or old man, are useful for many stories. An animal, such as a sheep, lion, or donkey, can also be used as these are frequently mentioned in well-known Bible stories.

Charts

A large chart helps students visualize lessons and understand them better. You can prepare these charts on poster board, newsprint, or construction paper. The lettering should be large enough for your class to see easily. Use colored markers to highlight key words. Charts can be made before class and thus save valuable teaching time. There are several styles of charts to choose from.

accordion chart

Use a long strip of shelf paper. Pleat it into even-sized pages. On each section mount one part of the picture or information you desire to teach. Unfold the pages as you teach.

flip chart

Bind or clamp several sheets of paper together at the top or left side. On each section mount one part of the picture or information you desire to teach. A summary chart can be done much the same way but with a small variation. Cut each page 2" shorter than the one below it and print a key word at the bottom of each page. As you flip the pages the summary can be seen at a glance.

sleeve chart

This aid allows you to reveal one section of the information at a time by pulling it out of a "sleeve." Print each segment on one line of a sheet of paper. Make a paper sleeve by using two sheets 1" wider and 1" longer than this information sheet. Tape or staple these two pieces together, leaving the top open.

strip chart

Print each part of the information on one line of your paper. Tape a strip of paper over each line. Remove the strips as you teach.

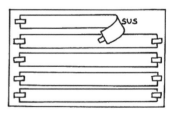

Codes

Codes can add interest to memory verses, lessons, and reviews. There are several basic types of codes. Once you understand the principle behind each type you can adapt them to your specific teaching aim and add pizzazz to your class.

symbol substitution
This method uses symbols, such as circles, squares, and triangles, instead of letters.

letter substitution
Another letter is substituted for the correct one in this code.
Example: Z = A Y = B W = C

number substitution
Here numbers are substituted for letters.
Example: 1 = A, 2 = B, 3 = C

Hebrew style
The Hebrew language is read from right to left. In this method write the words so that the sentence begins on the right side of the page instead of the left.
Example: .ELPMAXE NA SI SIHT

addition alphabet
The total of adding two numbers stands for a letter.
Example: 2 + 3 = A, 4 + 5 = B
Be sure to use a different number for each letter. If two totals are the same, the code won't work.
Example: 2 + 3 = A, 4 + 1 = B

subtraction alphabet
This code works the same as the addition alphabet, except that two numbers are subtracted instead of added.
Example: 7 - 2 = A, 12 - 8 = B

math alphabets
Still another variation of the two previous codes, these methods use some form of math to obtain the correct number substitute for the letter. You can have multiplication or division alphabets or use a combination of all four types of math problems. In all of these the same caution is extended—if two answers are the same, the code won't work.

grid-code alphabet
In this code the correct number for a letter is determined by its position in a grid. The vertical position determines the first number and the horizontal position determines the second number.
Example: 11 = A 12 = B

position code
Lines and dots are substituted for a letter. Example: $\vee$ = A,
$<$ = B

	1	2	3	4	5	6
1	A	B	C	D	E	F
2	G	H	I	J	K	L
3	M	N	O	P	Q	R
4	S	T	U	V	W	X
5	Y	Z	?	!	"	;
6	:	,	.			

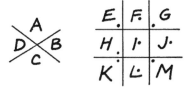

11

computer binary alphabet

A computer uses different combinations of two symbols , zero and one, to stand for letters. The code is limited to these two symbols which are repeated in different combinations.

Example: 101010 = A, 110101 = B, 010101 = C, 001100 = D

telephone dial

This code comes directly from your telephone dial to you. Look at a dial and you will see that one number stands for 3 different letters. The number 2 stands for A, B, and C. In order to help your students determine which letter the number stands for, use a small line to clarify the correct letter. A line to the left (\) can mean the letter in the first alphabetical position. A line to the right (/) means the letter in the last alphabetical position. A letter with no lines means the middle position.

Example: \2 = A, 2 = B, 2 = C/
          \7 = P, 7 = R, 7 = S/

Since the letters "Q" and "Z" are not given on the dial, you can use the number 0 with left and right lines for them.

letter change

In this method, little-used letters take the place of other letters. They are then changed to the correct letter.

Example: Change all X's to A's
           Z's to E's
           XPPLZ (APPLE) IDZXS (IDEAS)

mirror writing

Words are printed as they appear in a mirror. To help you write this code, print the letters correctly then look at them in a mirror or from the back side of the paper.

Contests

People are great competitors so use contests to promote memorization, bringing Bibles, completing the lesson, bringing visitors, etc. Classroom posters which use stickers are easily made. You can use reproducible or clip-art pictures as background patterns. All sorts of stickers are available to add details to these backgrounds. Rubber stamps can be used instead of stickers. (See RUBBER STAMPS.) Reproducible certificates are available to use as awards. (See the books *Award Certificates for Bible Memory, With Bible Verses,* and *For Almost All Occasions* by Standard Publishing.)

Craft Smock

Use these simple-to-make smocks whenever students are involved in messy projects. Cut a head hole in the center bottom of a

large plastic trash bag. Cut two arm holes in each side of the bag. Wipe the smocks clean with a damp cloth when finished using them and fold them up for later use.

Figures

chenille wire figures

Simple figures can be made from chenille wire. This wire can be formed into stick-figures by using different lengths of wire and twisting them together to make people, animals, or plants.

clothespin figures

Slip-over clothespins make good characters to act out Bible stories or plays. Use 3" of chenille wire and glue this far up in the slot for arms. Make a "V" shape of cardboard and insert this into the bottom of the slot for a stand. Draw a face on one side of the round top of the clothespin with felt tip markers. For a robe, cut a small cloth rectangle as long as the clothespin is from the "neck" down. Gather and tie this cloth firmly at the back of the figure's neck. Cut small slits for the wire arms and use yarn for a belt. Use small pieces of cloth for head coverings and aluminum foil, old jewelry, or sequins for crowns, necklaces, etc. Store these figures in a plastic zipper-bag.

paper figures

Several basic types of figures can be cut from paper.

folded paper figure

This is made by folding a piece of paper in half, drawing a figure and cutting it out. The center fold allows it to stand up. A basic animal pattern for use with young children is also illustrated. This can be varied by adding different heads and body markings.

An added tab on the bottom of a folded paper figure can make it stand better. Fold these tabs under the figure and lap them over one another. Glue or tape them in place.

dress-up figure

This stand-up figure can be a dress-up person so you can change the costumes for different Biblical characters or time periods. Draw a basic figure on poster board. Be sure to make the shoulders of the people wide enough so you can fold the clothes tabs over them! Color and cut the figure out. Cut two slots in the base of it. Make 2 base strips to allow the figure to stand up. Cut the slots in these base pieces the same width as the thickness of your poster board. Lay the figure flat and trace around it to be sure that the clothes will fit. Be sure to allow for fold-over tabs which will keep the clothes in place. Cut a slit in head gear and push the figure's head through carefully.

jointed cardboard figures

Make each section of the arms (such as upper and lower arm) separately. Color with markers or crayons and cut out. Overlap these sections at elbows, knees, etc. and attach with paper fasteners. Now the figure can kneel, pray, walk, etc. This works for animals as well as human figures.

File Folder Game

By gluing board games inside file folders you add sturdy foundations and convenience. A single page game can be glued to one inside page of the folder while a larger board game can be glued all the way across. A two-page board can be joined at the inside fold and covered with clear adhesive-plastic. For one page games you can glue the playing board to the inside front cover and a spinner to the inside back cover. Buttons, cardboard circles, or pennies can be used as playing pieces. These can be kept in a small plastic zipper bag which is stapled to the back cover. Any separate directions can be glued to the front cover. Descriptive pictures can be added if desired.

You can use folders for question and answer games. Make pockets of construction paper to hold the questions. Mount a piece of notebook paper on one page for writing answers. Cover this with clear adhesive-plastic so students can use a watercolor marker to write answers. Stick the marker in the question pocket. A variation on this method is to print a question on the page. The answer is printed below it and covered with a construction paper flap. Students raise the flap to find the answer. This works well when you want to introduce new information in a creative way.

By using colored folders instead of plain manila ones, you can add bright accents to the games and make them more appealing.

Finger Plays

We all talk with our hands. In this method children use their fingers and hands to act out words in a song, poem, or memory verse.

It provides needed movement for active young bodies and at the same time helps to fix the lesson in the child's mind. (See the book *Glove Puppets – Let Your Fingers Do the Talking* by Standard Publishing for more information on fingerplays for teaching Scripture.)

Fishing Poles

Children love to fish. This provides a unique way to review lessons or memory verses. Use a short length of dowel and tie a string on one end of it. Tie a small magnet to the other end of the string. Cut fish shapes from construction paper. Write a verse reference or question on each fish. Attach a paper clip on the fish and place them in a dry bowl. The child "fishes" and must say the verse or answer the question caught.

You can make a chain of paper clips to be a "stringer" for your fish. Punch a hole near the fish's mouth to hang it on the chain.

Flannelboards

The simplest board is made of heavy cardboard and felt. The felt can be cut to fit the cardboard and glued to it. A different color felt can be used to cover the back of the cardboard if desired. In this way you can have both a dark color (for night scenes or light-colored figures) and a light color (for day scenes or dark-colored figures).

Another method is to use cardboard and a slip-over flannel cover. Cut a piece of flannel big enough to cover the cardboard plus 1/2" longer and wider. This allows for 1/4" seams on all sides. Cut a piece of attractive print cloth the same size as flannel for the outside cover. Sew these two pieces together on three sides, leaving one short end open. Insert the cardboard and whipstitch cloth shut. This kind of cover allows you to replace the cardboard if it gets bent out of shape, or to wash the cover if it is dirty or needs fluffing up. Another option is to use flannel on both sides—one light colored and the other dark colored. If you choose to do this, be sure to place the dark color on the outside.

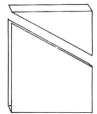

A 3-dimensional board can be made from a sturdy cardboard box. Cut one corner off the box as shown. Glue a piece of felt over the biggest flat surface of this corner. A folding flannelboard is good to have if you need a bigger board but are limited for storage space. Cut two equal size pieces of heavy cardboard. Connect these pieces with plastic tape, leaving room enough between to fold them together. Cover this board in the same manner as the flannelboard above. A cloth tab can be sewn into one end to hold the board closed. Velcro or a snap can be attached to this tab and a matching spot on the cover.

By having the board fold up, it can be stored in half the space. It also allows you to carry flannelgraph figures in it safely. These boards are lightweight and can be taken along for class outings or services at parks and camping areas. The boards can be varied in size and flannel colors. For example, use a black or dark blue for night scenes and a light, neutral color for daytime ones. These boards may need to have a sturdy piece of cardboard behind them when placed on some easels as they tend to bend inward at the middle.

Flannelgraph Backgrounds

Purchased backgrounds are often quite expensive, but you can make your own. Start by cutting a piece of flannel large enough to cover your flannelboard. Sketch in the scene with a washable fabric marker using a coloring book or picture as a guide. Because markers bleed easily on flannel, outline the main parts using a <u>fine-tip</u> permanent marker such as a Sharpie. The rest of the picture may be colored using crayons, permanent-ink markers, or fabric paints. To prevent fraying you can treat the edges of the flannel with a liquid like Fray Chek (Dritz) or a thin mixture of white glue. The glue will wash out; the Fray Check won't.

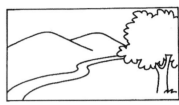

Flannelgraph Figures

Almost any picture can be made into a flannelgraph figure by gluing flannel remnants on the back. Or you can coat them with a layer of rubber cement. Allow the cement to dry before using on the board. These figures tend to stick to each other, so they need to be stored with wax paper or scrap paper between them.

Another method is by making figures on construction paper. (See "Visuals" in the HINTS section.) When you have colored your figure, sand it lightly on the back side with a medium grade of sandpaper until the construction paper feels roughed up and like flannel. Cut on the broad black outline. Round off corners and fill in back spaces with the black marker to make the figure easier to cut around. This also makes it less likely to tear than if it had sharp corners or small projections.

Pellon interfacing can also be used for figures. Use the sew-in kind that is rather firm on the surface. It is thin enough to trace through and can be colored on both sides so that figures can be used to face two directions. This eliminates the need for two separate figures. It is virtually tear resistant and adheres to a flannelboard well. Color with markers, crayons, or tempera paints. If you use crayons, turn the figure over or cover the crayon side with a cloth and iron it with a medium temperature iron to set the colors and make them brighter.

Felt also makes good flannelgraph figures. It is relatively inexpensive and readily available in a wide variety of colors. This works where the picture is basically one color, such as fruit, flowers, or animals. It adheres to the flannelboard easily.

You can add wiggle eyes, glitter, and fake fur or cloth accents to any of the above materials for extra appeal.

Flash Cards

Mount pictures from coloring books, magazines, recycled Sunday-school materials, etc. on construction paper pages. These pages can be shapes that are made to convey an idea from the story, such as an ark for Noah or a cross for Easter. The cover page should have details of the shape and the title on it.

Punch holes in the backgrounds and put the cards together with metal rings or plastic chicken rings to make them easier to handle.

Flip Book

Use large size 5" x 7" or 4" x 6" index cards. Cut several in half. Glue recycled Sunday-school pictures on half of these cut cards and write matching descriptions on the other half. Leave two cards whole for the front and back covers. Attach the cut cards to these covers with metal rings, placing the pictures and the descriptions side-by-side in a scrambled order for lesson review. You can also use this kind of book for matching questions and answers; verses and references; people and character descriptions.

Games

spinners

Draw a circle on a square piece of paper. Divide the circle into as many sections as you desire. Number each section. For younger students you can use colors instead of numbers to indicate different section values. Mount the paper square on heavy poster board or cardboard. Cover the spinner with clear adhesive-plastic. Use a paper clip on a paper fastener and push it through the center of the spinner. Bend this fastener loosely so there is a space between the tip of the fastener and the surface of the circle. The clip will then spin easily. Taping the fastener on the back side will keep it in place.

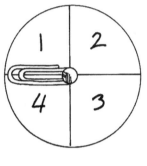

hamburger match-up

A good matching game can be made by filling a styrofoam sandwich container from a fast food restaurant with several colored construction paper hamburgers, buns, cheese, etc. Place different information on each part. For example a memory verse game:

Burger = text
Cheese = Bible book
Bun top = chapter
Bun bottom = verse

dunkin' doughnuts

This is also a matching game. Make several cardboard doughnuts. Place these, along with the same number of small paper cups, in a doughnut box or paper sack. Students will match items (question and answer; verse and reference; Bible characters and descriptions; etc.) by "dunking doughnuts" into the matching cups.

pick-a-card review

This review game works well for memory verses. Write the verse references on a number of 3"x 5" index cards. Punch holes in the center of each 3" end. Use a 3'- 4' long piece of yarn or string and thread a brightly colored button in the middle of it. Fold the cards in half, with the writing inside, and string half of these on either side of the button. Form the class into two teams. One player from each team holds an end of the string. The first player pulls off a card and reads the reference. The opposing team must give the verse. If it is unable to do so, the first team has a chance. The team that says the verse correctly keeps the card. At the end of the game the team with the most cards wins. This can also be done with questions and answers for a lesson review.

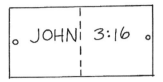

scrambled eggs

For a memory verse review, write the verses and references on strips of paper. Cut words or phrases apart. Put them in plastic Easter eggs and place these in an egg carton. Students select an egg and reassemble the verse in the correct order.

treat on a stick

Yet another matching game, this one uses a number of colored sucker-size poster board circles and craft sticks or tongue depressors. In a memory verse review, place the text on the candy and the reference on the stick. The stick is then matched to the sucker. For a Biblical person game the candy can be the description and the stick the name of the Bible character. You can vary this game by using different shapes for the treats, such as popsicles or candy apples instead of suckers.

*(See the book *Let the Games Begin!* by Standard Publishing for more information on making reproducible creative games for teaching Scripture.)

hidden-object puzzles

Children love hidden-object puzzles and they are a good way to introduce a lesson. Draw or trace a simple outline of the item you want to hide on a piece of paper. It works best if you don't place it in the center of the page. Draw lines, in the space around it, that are similar to the shape of this object . These additional lines should resemble the same curves and angles as that of your hidden figure. Fill the rest of the page with similar jigsaw lines. This helps the chosen object to blend in with its surroundings. Be careful not to add so many lines that you confuse the puzzle.

To enable younger students to find the figure more easily, place a tiny mark, such as an "x," in one corner of every part of the puzzle except the ones which make up the hidden object. They then color these "x" sections leaving the featured shape white. If these segments are each made a different color, it gives the effect of a stained glass window.

invisible inks

These inks use common ingredients to write secret messages. They are relatively easy to use and the mystery involved in revealing the message adds to their appeal. This kind of secret works well to introduce a subject, such as the hidden ways Satan works in the world or the way early Christians had to identify themselves and pass messages during persecution.

Use any of the following as ink: onion juice, lemon juice, orange juice, apple juice, milk, 7-Up, vinegar, or 1 teaspoon of baking soda, sugar, or salt dissolved in 2 teaspoons of water.

The message is written on white paper with one of the inks using a small brush, finger, or toothpick. Once the ink has dried the message is invisible. By holding the paper up to a light bulb or over a toaster, the message appears again in brown letters.

Lacing Pictures

Glue recycled magazine, calendar, or Sunday-school pictures to cardboard backgrounds. Cover these pictures with clear adhesive-plastic. Use a paper drill or punch to make evenly spaced holes around the parts of the picture you want to emphasize. Use shoe laces or yarn for lacing. If you use yarn, dip the ends in white glue and shape them to points before the glue dries for easier lacing.

Young children can handle shaped lacing pictures best. Cut out a large shape and punch holes around the edges.

A plastic lid also makes a simple lacing card. Glue a simple picture on the lid and punch holes around the picture's outline.

Learning Centers

These specialized teaching sites offer students the opportunity to explore in depth specific topics or areas of study. All that is really needed to set up a learning center is a small space in a room and a table easily accessible to students. Learning centers can be arranged around almost any kind of theme. Some good subjects for learning centers are as follows: books; games; musical tapes and records; drama and puppets; missions; nature; arts and crafts; review activities; memory work; Bible study; prayer; creative writing; role-plays; student achievements; current events; or even refreshments. Try a "surprise" center where you can feature any activity that reinforces your lesson aim. For example, you could have a pre-recorded story, video presentation, or mystery guest at this center.

Display the items to be featured along with notepaper, pencils, markers, etc. Arrange comfortable chairs or cushions around the table. Students are allowed to visit the center and explore the featured theme. To maintain interest, change the centers often and switch students from one center to another.

Magnetic Board

Use a metal cookie sheet, piece of sheet metal, or a child's magnetic board from a store for the board. Back your visuals with small pieces from a magnetic strip. These strips are available wherever crafts are sold. They come in a small roll and can be cut into any desired lengths.

Mailbox

Use an old mailbox to bring God's Word to life. Repaint the box in bright colors. You can use decals or stencils to decorate it. Before class put the memory verse in an envelope, address it to your students, add a sticker "stamp" and place it in the box. Pull it out and read it during class. This really helps young students see that the Bible is God speaking to us today.

Mail Call

All students love to receive mail. Use the mailman to deliver postcards to congratulate, advise, or encourage students. Try using personalized cards to add that special touch. (See following section, PERSONALIZED CARDS.)

Matching Board

This is an excellent tool for reviewing a lesson. Cut two equal size rectangular pieces of poster board. Cover the surface of one piece with clear adhesive-plastic. Attach 10-12 paper fasteners in two columns about 2" from the outside edges of this piece of poster board. Leave a 2" space between these columns. Bend the fasteners loosely so there is a space between the tip of the fastener and the surface of the poster board. Glue the second piece of poster board over the back side of the first piece, covering the paper fastener ends. Write the question on the left side of the top board and the matching answers in scrambled order on the right side. Use a permanent-ink marker as this board will get a lot of handling. Remove ink (see "Adhesive Plastic" in HINTS) and change items as desired. Items are matched by stretching sturdy rubber bands between fasteners.

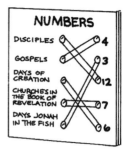

Mazes

Mazes are good ways to reinforce memory verses. They are usually made in a geometric pattern of some sort. Most are set in a block, such as a square, rectangle, or circle of letters. Using graph paper, which is printed in squares, is a must when making these mazes.

word search

In this maze a number of words are hidden within a square or rectangle of superfluous letters that do not apply to those particular words. The words can be hidden across—backwards or forwards, up, down, or diagonally. Care should be taken that extra neighboring letters do not spell other words or confuse students.

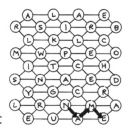

circle-line word search

This maze got its start from an engineering form used for drafting. Letters are placed in circles joined by lines. The words can go forward, backward, up, down, or twist around. This activity is geared to older students.

As above, care should be taken that adjoining, extra letters do not spell other words or confuse students.

arrows

In this maze use only the letters that spell the desired words. It is based on a square or rectangle but uses arrows to direct students to the next letter. Words can be distinguished by providing blanks which indicate how many letters are in each word.

doors

Here the base maze is set up like the Arrow one above. But instead of using arrows to direct students to letters, this maze has them go through open "doors" to the next letter.

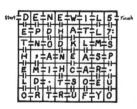

spiral

The letters begin at the outside of a spiral and wind inward so that the end of the message is at the center. Use only the necessary letters. Students can either decide when a word ends or be given blank-space hints as in Arrow Mazes.

circle

The essential letters are placed around the circumference of a circle. They are usually set up so that you have to go around the circle twice to figure out the message. Thus the letters are positioned so that every other letter is used each time around. For the first time around the circle, place the letters in spots 1, 3, 5, etc. The second time around the letters are in spots 2, 4, 6, etc.

path

Here a regular path maze is used with both necessary and non-essential words being placed in it. All non-essential words are located in paths that come to dead ends while the correct words are placed, in order, on the only path from the beginning through the maze to its destination.

Memo Board

A portable memo board can be made from sturdy cardboard with a cover made of a jumbo clear plastic zipper-bag. The cardboard provides a firm writing surface. Cover it with white paper for ease in seeing the writing. Insert the cardboard into the bag and close. Use watercolor markers on the plastic and erase with a damp cloth. You can also slip maps inside the plastic and use markers to trace routes such as Jesus' travels or Paul's missionary journeys.

Mini-Lessons

Children act out in play the things they have experienced—a visit to the doctor, going to school, etc. Capitalize on this characteristic by using a children's teaching packet as a reward for good work. They can be encouraged to "teach" friends and family members. Make a mini-lesson using a 9" x 12" manila envelope and these items:

mini-flannelboard

Use an 8 1/2" x 11" piece of cardboard. A back from a school writing tablet works perfectly. Glue flannel or felt to this base.

mini-lesson

Recycle old Sunday-school materials or extra figures you've made. Prepare them for the flannelboard using one of the methods described in the previous flannelgraph figure section.

mini-song

Many familiar songs are available in miniature form from Child Evangelism Fellowship, Warrenton, MO. If not available, make one of your own using pictures or shapes to illustrate key words. (See REBUS.)

Mix-N-Match Book

Use this book to teach and review memory verses or review stories. Use a three-ring notebook and 3" x 5" index cards. Punch a hole in the center of one short side of each card. To teach or review a memory verse, divide it into three sections and print one part on each of three cards. To review a story choose three key words or phrases and write one word or phrase on three separate cards. A variation of this is to use the names of three important characters from the story. Place each section on a separate ring of the notebook, stacking them in a scrambled order. Let students find the three matching cards.

Mobiles

Mobiles are great room decorations and easy to make. They can be used to review lessons or memory verses. To review a lesson or unit, choose pictures that remind students of what was studied. There are several options for the mobile base: an embroidery hoop, poster board strip made into a circle, crossed drinking straws or short pieces of dowels. Hang the pictures from the base, being careful to balance them around it for easy movement by air currents. You can also use a large picture as the base and devise your own system of hanging pictures from one another to balance the mobile.

A verse mobile can be done in the same manner, substituting words or phrases for pictures. You can use the reference as the base.

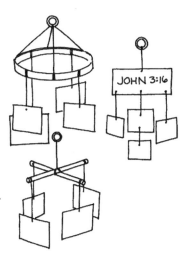

Models

Models of Bible-times buildings can help children better understand what life was like for the people in their lessons. Homes were very plain. You can make them out of old boxes or poster board. Most buildings were shaped like square boxes. Outside stairways to rooftops can be made by pleating construction paper or tagboard accordion-style and gluing this to the box building. A glue gun works well here as the steps are hard to hold in place with white glue. Use small pictures of Bible people to illustrate daily life. Glue pictures of faces or figures to the windows or doorways of buildings. Stand-up figures can be made by gluing pictures to poster board backs and allowing for fold-back bases.

(*Bible-Times Village to Make* and *Tabernacle Model to Make* are also available from Standard Publishing. These include stand-up visuals of people from that era engaged in everyday activities.)

Mystery Boxes

Recycle a round oatmeal carton and a man's worn-out sock into a mystery box. Remove the box lid. Cut the foot off the sock and stretch the bottom of the cuff over the box top. Tape it on with strapping or plastic tape. Cover the box with attractive adhesive-plastic. Place mystery objects in the box through the cuff opening. Choose objects that correlate with the lesson. For example, a stone for Jacob's pillow or David's sling. Children reach inside the box and try to guess what the mystery object is. This provides a natural opening for the teacher to introduce the lesson.

A shoe box can also make a mystery box. Cut a hole large enough for a student's hand in one end of the box. Put on the lid. After placing the mystery object in the box, slip a large rubber band around the box and lid to prevent peeking.

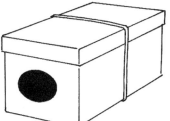

Object Lessons

Almost any object can be used for a lesson. For example: gold, food, a compass, a light, weapons, tools, a mirror, seeds, water, musical instruments, milk, medicine, etc. can all be used to illustrate teachings from the Bible. Jesus used common objects, such as seed, birds, and flowers, to teach His followers. Keep your eyes open for any object that reminds you of God or something He has used to speak to you. There are also many books of simple object talks on the market.

Peep Boxes

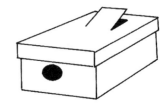

Any box with a lid will do. Cut a small hole in one end of the box for the child to look through. Glue a picture or figure inside the box on the opposite end from this hole. Cut a small hinged window in the top of the lid for a skylight above the picture.

Pegboards

This is masonite with evenly spaced, pre-drilled holes. It can be mounted on a wall as in a library or classroom or made into a portable board. Use the hooks that are made for it and display books or heavy game boards.

Personalized Cards

Use these special cards for students who are sick, absent, or are celebrating special occasions. Cut out cartoon-style pictures from gift wrap or magazines. Glue these to typing paper cut in note-paper size. Add your own speech balloons personalizing the situation and mail to students. For example, a picture of a kitten and a puppy playing together might have two speech balloons reading: "I sure missed Chad in Sunday school today." "Me too! I hope he isn't sick but will hurry back next week." Sign the card and mail it in a regular size envelope.

Pictures

add-a-feel picture

You can give any picture an added dimension by gluing on pieces of fabric for clothing, fake fur scraps for animals, real seeds for fruit, vegetables, etc. Small children especially enjoy this addition.

draw-your-own pictures

Even non-artists can try stick figures or circle-line drawings. Most figures are basically combinations of common shapes, such as circles, oblongs, triangles, etc. Check with art or hobby stores for ideas. You don't have to be a professional artist. Children relate well to those of us who draw very simply as they do!

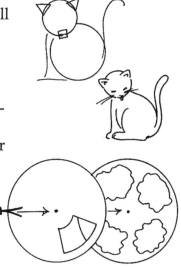

picture wheel

Cut two poster board or cardboard circles the same size. Cut a small section out of one circle to form a window. On the bottom circle, glue the pictures to be viewed. Place the window wheel over the picture wheel and secure both wheels in the center with a paper fastener. The wheel may be turned to each picture. Picture wheels can also be used to view memory verses or prayer reminders.

Play Dough

A simple, easy-to-store play dough can be made using the following ingredients: 1 1/2 C salt, 1 1/2 C water, 3 C flour.

Mix these ingredients together. The mixture should be the consistency of bread dough. If it is sticky, simply add more flour. Divide the dough into small portions and add a few drops of food coloring to make different colors. Place it in a plastic bag or tightly-covered container. Store the dough in the refrigerator. (See "Dough Art," CRAFTS, for many more recipes.)

Playhouse

This playhouse can be used very effectively as a teaching tool by giving children an opportunity to learn about life in other times and cultures. It is made to fit on a square table, such as a folding card table.

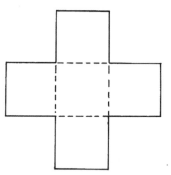

Measure your table top and add seam allowance on all four sides to determine your pattern. Cut five squares of felt from this pattern. Sew one square to each of the four sides of the fifth square. Leave the sides of these four squares open. You now have a drop-cover for the table.

Decorate one of the four sides to look like a Bible-times home. You can do this by using permanent-ink or fabric markers or gluing on felt windows, doors, etc. Each side can be done differently if desired. For example, you might do one side as a Bible-times home, one as a Bible-times jail, one as an African hut, and one as a Japanese home. This would provide for several Bible lessons as well as some on missions. Children can crawl in and out and pretend they are living in one of the "houses."

If you would like to add some basic teaching activities, you can print or pin to the tabletop "roof" some guides, such as these:

Who lives here?

How do they earn a living?

What would you eat if you lived here?

25

What toys would you play with if you lived here?

Tell a story about someone who lived here.

You could even place magazines or catalogs and children's scissors on the "roof" with instructions like: "Find and cut out a picture of something that belongs in this house."

This playhouse folds up and stores easily.

Pocket Chart

This aid uses heavy paper, folded and stapled to heavy cardboard. It can be used to hold figures for a three-dimensional look or teaching cards for a memory verse. A good size is made by using a 24" x 30" piece of tagboard. The width is 24" and the length 30". Make a fold 4 1/2" from one end. Allow 1" between it and the next 4 1/2" fold. This size will make five 4 1/2" folds and one 2" fold. Use a piece of heavy cardboard 20" high by 24" wide to make the backboard. Staple the folded pocket piece to this. If desired, you can use the back piece of the chart as an extra flannelboard by gluing on flannel or felt. It can also become a chalk or white board by adding these special adhesive-plastics.

Posters

You can use posters to decorate a room, publicize special events, or reinforce lessons. Recycle pictures from magazines or draw your own. Use letter stencils or rub-on letters if printing is difficult for you.

Puppet Stages

You can construct stages from a variety of simple objects.

box stages

Small boxes make good stages for teaching. Cut the flaps off the box. Cut out holes for the puppets to come through. Flaps will allow your puppets to pop up from unexpected areas. Decorate the box with paints, markers, cloth, silk flowers, etc.

An appliance box makes a large, classroom-sized stage. Students can stand up in these and remain hidden from the audience. Cut out one side of the box. Now the center section of the box forms the front of the stage and the other two sections, the fold-back wings. Cut a window in the upper 1/3 of the center section. Decorate this. Hang a curtain across the stage if desired.

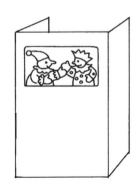

flat tray stage

This makes an individual-sized stage that hangs around the neck of the puppeteer and allows him to use two puppets. Use or cut

26

down a box so that the sides are about 4" high. Cut out two circles 2" apart on the center bottom of the box. This is where the puppets will appear. Punch two holes 3 1/2" apart in each of the two shorter sides. Use two lengths of rope to hang the stage around the puppeteer's neck. Thread each end of one rope through the two front holes. Knot them inside to hold them in place. Trim the stage as desired. Hang the stage over your neck and bring the puppets up through the holes.

table stage

Stand a folding table on its side in a doorway with the legs open for support. Operate the puppets from behind and hold them over the tabletop.

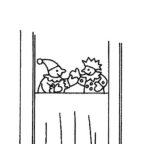

doorway stage

Tack a towel, curtain, or cloth to either side of a doorway. Puppeteers are positioned behind this barrier and hold the puppets above it.

Puppets

There are almost as many kinds of puppets as there are the number of people who enjoy them. Puppets are great teaching tools because they are so versatile. A puppet can: introduce a story; teach a memory verse; review a lesson; teach a song; lead a game; make an announcement; help a child deal with his feelings and problems; aid in discipline. You don't have to be a ventriloquist to use puppets. You can have the puppet whisper in your ear and you do the "interpreting." Or you can pre-record plays or dialogues incorporating other people's voices besides your own. This saves your having to read from a script and handle the puppet at the same time.

Although puppets can be purchased, they are easy to make. Since the audience is at a distance from the puppets, remember to use bright colors! Here are some simple kinds of puppets you can make. Try doing puppet plays at a local fair, nursing homes, hospitals, or camping areas for outreach projects.

box puppets

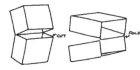

An individual-serving cereal box makes a nice size puppet. Remove the paper cover. Cut the box in half, leaving one edge connected. Fold the box over, leaving the open sections on the outside. Reinforce this fold on both sides with plastic tape. Glue a head on the closed ends of the box as shown. Slip your fingers into the open sections to move the puppet's mouth.

dancing stick puppets

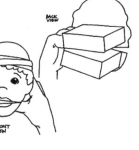

Glue the head and body portion of the figure to a craft stick or tongue depressor. Punch holes in the body where the arms and legs would be. Glue a hand to one end of a piece of yarn. Thread yarn back through one of the arm holes and out the front of the other arm hole. Glue the second hand to the end of this piece of yarn. Repeat the procedure for the feet. Tape the yarn to the back of the stick to keep it even.

finger puppets

One kind uses a sturdy paper figure with holes cut where the legs or arms would be. Mount the figure on poster board for greater durability. Insert your pointer and middle fingers to make the puppet walk, run, jump, or wave.

Another kind of finger puppet is also made of paper. Draw or mount the character in the middle of a strip long enough to wrap around finger. Tape or glue the end of the strip together to form a tube.

glove puppets

One glove can hold an entire cast of characters for a play. Use pom-poms and felt to construct the puppets. Glue these figures to the ends of the fingers. Although you can cut the fingers off and use only that portion of the glove, you will discover that it's much easier to slip on an entire glove for a play than several tiny puppets. If you use the glove, you can also glue scenery on the hand portion and add detail to your story. Velcro can also be attached to the glove and puppets so you can change the figures without having to have a separate glove for each story. (See the book *Glove Puppets – Let Your Fingers Do the Talking* by Standard Publishing for more information on glove puppets.)

mitt puppets

All mitt puppets are based on a common design. They vary in hand size and can be fashioned into many characters. Felt is probably the best material for these puppets as it offers you the option of gluing rather than sewing, although cloth can be used as well. Cut two mitt pieces. If you use glue, the puppet can be assembled right side out. When sewing, place the right sides of the material together and sew the seams. Turn right side out and decorate. Use wiggle eyes, felt, markers, embroidery, or fabric paints to add features and/or body details to animals. Yarn or fake fur makes good hair. Use your thumb and little finger to operate the arms and your other three fingers inside the head.

moving mouth puppets

Patterns for these complicated puppets are available through craft or commercial pattern companies. They are large, muppet-like puppets and require a good knowledge of sewing techniques.

paper bag puppets

Lunch bags make good puppets. Most paper bag puppets use only the head, but you can use the entire figure if you make the head larger than normal. Split the puppet so that the top part of the head is glued on the bottom flap of the bag. Mount the rest of the puppet on the side of the bag, making sure to line up the mouth. Bend four fingers and use them inside the folded flap to make the puppet talk.

paper plate puppets

Plain white paper plates can be used to make head puppets. Use the underside of the plate for the face. Add features and hair by using markers or adding pieces cut from paper, yarn, felt, or fake fur. Sectioned plates make great animal puppets. Glue a poster board strip across the inside center of the plate so you can slip the puppet on your hand.

pot holder puppets

This square fabric pot holder makes puppet heads only. Stitch each end of a 3 1/2" piece of 1/2" wide elastic to the back of the pot holder to slip hand into when holding the puppet. Use wiggle eyes, felt, markers, or fabric paints to add features.

shadow puppet

These simple puppets were probably enjoyed by people as early as Bible times. The outline figures were cut from leather and had vertical rods attached to the feet. They had no moving parts. A storyteller sat by a campfire and moved the puppets so that they cast silhouette shadows on the walls of the tent. The audience sitting on the other side of the tent was delighted by the combination of story and visuals.

You can duplicate these oldest of puppets by making simple paper silhouettes and mounting them on thin dowels or short lengths of heavy floral or stovepipe wire. Place them between a screen or sheet and a bright light. The puppet's shadow is thrown on the screen and viewed by the audience on the other side.

A variation can be made by attaching the rods to the hands and leaving the legs to swing freely. Make the legs in two sections—hip to knee and knee to foot. Attach these sections with paper fasteners, allowing the legs to move loosely as the puppet is operated.

sock puppets

Socks make inexpensive and fun puppets. Simply slip your hand and arm into a sock with your thumb in the heel so it pokes out under the foot. Presto! You have the basic puppet. Now add facial features and hair, using buttons, markers, yarn, fake fur, etc. Place these additions on the sock and study their effect before gluing or sewing them on. That way you can change them easily.

spoon puppets

Use plastic or wooden spoons for these little characters. Permanent-ink markers or paint make the features on the rounded back of the spoon. Hair, ears, etc. can be made of felt or yarn and glued on. Simple costumes can be constructed of strips of gathered cloth fastened around the spoon handle.

stick puppets

A figure is glued to a craft stick or tongue depressor. Use pictures from magazines or old Sunday-school lessons. In most cases the figure is mounted on the top of the stick and moved from below, but it can also mounted on the bottom and maneuvered from above.

tube puppets

Cut a bathroom tissue tube into a finger-length section. Mount a paper or felt character on the tube. Slip the tube over your finger and wiggle it to bring the puppet to life.

A variation of this puppet can be made by adding short lengths of dowels to the inside of the tube at the top. This allows you to manipulate the puppets from above and you can set them down into a stage setting.

Another style of tube puppet can also be made. Cut the tube 1/2" longer than finger length. Cut a row of 1/2" long slits evenly spaced around the tube. Bend this fringe down to form hair. Draw a face below the hair.

Puzzles

Glue a picture to lightweight cardboard or poster board. Cut this apart in jigsaw puzzle shapes. Adapt this to the age of your students. Make a few big, easy-to-fit-together pieces for young children. Cut more, smaller pieces for older students. Puzzles can even grow with your students by cutting the large pieces into smaller ones as the children gain manipulative skills. Select pictures appropriate to the lesson. They may be covered with clear adhesive-plastic for protection before cutting or even velcro backed for use on the flannelboard.

Quick Frames

A frame sets off a picture and makes it more attractive. Here are two versions of frames you can make quickly for classroom use.

pie pan frame

Mark the bottom of an aluminum pie pan into eight sections. Cut these sections from the center to the sides. Using a pencil, roll each pan "slice" out to the sides. Glue or staple the uncut edge of the pan to the picture.

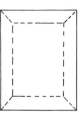

poster board frame

Use a piece of poster board about 2″ longer and wider than the picture you want to frame. Center the picture on the poster board and draw around it. Score and fold the poster board from the corners of this shape to the corners of the poster board. Then score and fold in along the straight lines of the shape. Attach the picture inside this 3-D frame with tape, rubber cement, or pins.

You can make several varieties of this frame. By cutting out the center of the frame, you can tape larger or odd-sized pictures behind it. Pictures can be changed easily if you glue a top-opening plastic sheet protector inside the frame. To obtain a completely different look, reverse the frame and mount your picture on the back side of it instead of the front.

Question Mark

Even children who are just learning to read love to use this method of review. Team them up with a more advanced reader or read the question for them yourself.

Cut a large question mark from lightweight wood or heavy cardboard. The period-dot at the bottom can be joined right to the top part of the mark and cut all as one piece. Drill or poke holes along the question mark big enough to insert rolled up paper questions. Write out each question on a slip of paper and roll it to fit into the holes in the question mark. Hold out the question mark and allow your students to pick their own questions and answer them. If you desire, you can modify this idea by drawing the mark on a large sheet of poster board. Instead of cutting it out, prop the poster board sheet up by adding a small piece of poster board on the back as an easel. Score this easel piece 1″ from the top and bend the rest of the piece outward. Center it and line it up evenly with the bottom of the question mark sheet. Glue it in place.

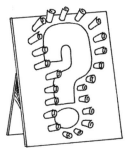

For a team review, make two small question marks the same size with the same number of holes in each. Make two copies of the questions and place them in different positions in each question mark. Divide the class into two teams and play as before—drawing out and answering questions, but now against each other.

Rebus Charts

A rebus chart allows pictures or symbols to be substituted for key words in a sentence. You can use a rebus for teaching a memory verse or illustrating a song. Write the desired "background" words on a piece of poster board or newsprint, leaving a space for the words that will be substituted with pictures. Glue or draw pictures in their proper places.

Rhythm Band Instruments

Young children love rhythm bands. The instruments are easily made from inexpensive materials.

bell stick

Wooden slip-over clothespins form the base. String two jingle bells on yarn or string and attach them around the base of the rounded top of the clothespin.

tambourines

Glue two paper plates together. Before gluing, place a handful of pebbles, rice, dried peas or beans inside. Decorate the outside edge by punching holes and tying jingle bells or colorful yarn fringe in the holes.

You can also use two aluminum pie pans instead of paper plates. In this instance, eliminate the gluing and simply fasten the pieces together with the yarn or bells.

shakers

Place pebbles, rice, dried peas or beans, or small jingle bells inside two paper or plastic cups. Tape these cups together with plastic tape.

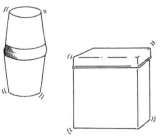

Small containers, such as those used for Band-Aids or spice, also make good shakers. Besides the items mentioned above, beads, pasta, or buttons can also be used as noisemakers.
Bathroom tissue or paper towel tubes are yet another type of container for shakers. Use any of the same materials for the inside noise makers. Seal the ends of the tubes with cardboard circles. Draw around the end of the tube on the cardboard. Cut this seal slightly larger than the circle. Make several slits from the outer edge as far inside as to the circle line. Place the cardboard over the tube and tape the slits down around it with plastic tape.

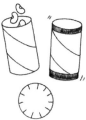

sand blocks

Use two blocks of wood about the size of chalkboard erasers. Staple coarse sandpaper over one surface of each block. Rub the sandpaper surfaces together.

drums

Containers, such as oatmeal boxes or cottage cheese cartons, make good drums. Glue or tape the lids in place. Use a dowel or wooden spoon as a drumstick.

rhythm sticks

Use two 9" long wooden dowels. Hit these together to play. Be sure the dowel ends are smooth, so students won't get hurt.

tube kazoo

Cut an 8" length of paper towel tube. Cover this with patterned adhesive-plastic. Make the plastic long enough to tuck inside the tube on one end. At one end of the tube punch a 1/4" hole. Cut a wax paper square a few inches larger than the end of the tube. Fasten this over the end of the tube without the tucked-in plastic and tape it in place. Punch a 1/4" hole in the tube above the wax paper. Students hum into the open end of the tube to play this kazoo.

comb kazoo

An even simpler type of kazoo can be made by placing a piece of tissue or wax paper over the teeth of a comb and humming on it.

Rubber Stamps

Rubber stamps are good tools for reinforcing learning. They can be used instead of stickers to reward students for good work as well as to encourage them to improve skills. Look around in an office supply store or a bookstore for stamps that have messages, such as "Good work," "You're improving," "Happy Birthday," and "I love you."

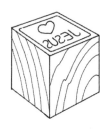

You can also make "rubber" stamps using Styrofoam from fast-food containers. Use a knife to cut the Styrofoam into a circle, triangle, square, or other basic shape. Glue this shape to a block of wood with white glue. Let dry. Draw a design on paper that will fit the Styrofoam stamp. Trace this pattern on the stamp using a sharp pencil. This will indent the surface. Remove the paper pattern and deepen the indention with the pencil point or a pin. This indented surface will not pick up ink from the stamp pad and show up white. While not a permanent stamp, this Styrofoam imitation will last for many uses. Try them out with different colors of ink. Stamp pads are available in rainbow colors as well as primary colors. You can also use tempera paints.

Sandbox

A large cake pan or sturdy cardboard box lined with aluminum foil can be used for a teaching sandbox. The metal pan or foil allows sand to be moistened to form hills and hold shapes. You can add to this scenery by using artificial flowers, small mirrors as lakes, and sticks for trees. The addition of chenille wire figures or pictures glued to craft sticks stuck in the sand will make your scene complete.

Sign Language

This method uses the same idea as finger plays, but is a recognized international language for the hearing or speech impaired. This makes it very useful for carry-over into everyday life. It utilizes hand movements for words or phrases.

Sound Effects

Sound effects add realism to plays, programs, and stories. Tape them for use or have your students participate in the fun of bringing life to familiar Bible stories.

thunder
Shake a large tin sheet backward and forward.

rain
To make it sound like rain beating on the window, scatter uncooked rice or pasta onto a cake pan or cookie sheet.

crackling flames
Crumple a piece of cellophane paper into a ball.

birds singing
Rub a wet cork over the side of a glass bottle.

marching feet
Put a large number of stones inside a tin can. Place the lid on the can and shake it up and down.

horses' hooves
Use two sturdy plastic glasses. Knock first one end, then the other of one glass down on a table top. "Clop" the second glass after the other. Increase your speed.

Story Aprons

Aprons make wonderful aids for telling stories. Their pockets can hide items used in the story. Some aprons can even be used for a flannelboard.

pocket apron
Use an apron with several large pockets. Before telling the story or reviewing a lesson, hide suitable items in the pockets. Pockets can be used for an object lesson, puppets, or flannelgraph figures. Items can be pulled out of the pockets at the appropriate time in the story. For a review, children can

guess the contents of the pocket and explain their connection with the lesson.

flannelgraph apron

A background apron can be made out of flannel or felt. You can make it out of strips by using blue for the top 1/3 of the apron and brown or green for the bottom 2/3. Back this apron with heavy-weight interfacing and tie it on loosely. Flannelgraph figures can be placed directly on the apron.

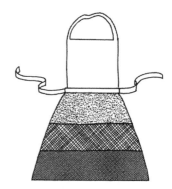

sandwich apron

This is a variation of the flannelgraph apron but made for greater versatility. Choose both a light and dark color of brushed nylon, flannel, or fleece. Each color will be used for 1/2 of the apron. Use a carpenter-style pattern as a base. However, instead of cutting different front and back pieces, make both pieces like the front pattern. Make the neck opening large enough to slip over your head and leave both sides open. Add a large pocket the full length of the apron bottom and divide it into 2 or 3 smaller pockets. Velcro strips sewn on the waist will close the apron. Use the hook side of the velcro for front sides of the apron and the loop part for the back sides. This will allow the apron to be adjusted for different sizes. Flannelgraph figures can be kept in the pockets and placed directly on the apron.

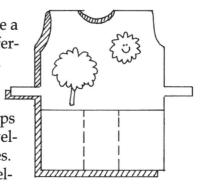

Story Cushions

Carpet samples or remnants make good cushions for children who sit on the floor for story times. Cut the pieces into 13" squares. Keep them in a box or corner of the room for easy access.

Another way to make cushions is by using upholstery material or sturdy fabric. Cut pieces about 27" x 14". Fold them in half, wrong side out, and sew 1/2" seams on the two long sides. Turn right side out and stuff with several layers of newspapers. Fold the ends in 1/2" and top-stitch shut. These cushions also make nice chair cushions for adults when folding chairs are cold or hard.

Still another method is to take a jumbo size plastic zipper bag and fill it with shredded newspaper. Zip bag shut. Cover this with another jumbo zip-bag, placing zipper at the opposite end of the first bag. Zip this bag shut and use plastic tape to be sure the bag won't open when used.

Styrofoam Board

This teaching aid is used for telling stories. Use a sheet of Styrofoam and lay it flat on the table. Prop up a background picture at the back of the Styrofoam by using the method described previously in the section QUESTION MARK. Tape craft sticks or toothpicks to the backs of story figures and move them about by sticking them into the Styrofoam.

Surprise Balls

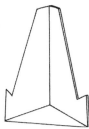

This teaching aid is adaptable to many purposes. You can use it to review Bible stories or memory verses, assign classroom duties, or remember missionaries or prayer requests. Before class, write whatever information you want to use on little slips of paper. Fold them several times and cover them one by one by winding them into a large ball of yarn. Allow students to take turns unwinding the ball to find the next question or message.

Tabletop Easel

Use a knife to cut a corner out of a sturdy cardboard box. Curve the ends up as shown. To make the easel more attractive, cover it with adhesive-plastic. You can use this handy easel to hold pictures, small flannelboards, or books.

Tape Recorder

A teacher can use a tape recorder in many ways. You can pre-record a story or lesson using people to play different characters. Bring all the wonderful sounds of God's world, such as birds' singing, thunder, frogs' croaking, etc., into the classroom. Illustrate the struggles of everyday life by recording the frustrations of getting ready for church on Sunday morning. Or use the sounds of crowds cheering at a ball game to give meaning to Paul's illustration in Hebrews 11 of the heroes and heroines of faith cheering
us on to victory. Invite a mystery guest into your classroom via tape recorder. The guest can tell about him/herself as though he/she were a Bible character and let the class discover who that person is.

People are eager to hear their own voice so use the tape recorder to capture your students saying their memory verses or acting out the characters in a role play or skit.

Tape a classroom lesson to send to a homebound student. He will feel included and less cut-off from his classmates.

Teaching Cubes

This aid can be used to tell a story or to review a lesson or several memory verses. Use the illustration as a pattern to make the box out of poster board. It should be about 9" square. Cut only on the solid lines and fold on the dotted lines.

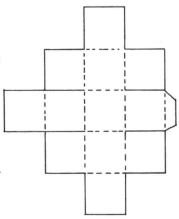

Display one picture on each side of the box. Place any additional teaching items, such as puppets, object lessons, or figures, inside the box. Pull them out to reinforce the story. Review questions or references for memory verses can be substituted for story pictures.

If you use the same size pictures all or most of the time, cut slits in the sides of the box so you can insert the corners of the pictures. If you will be using pictures of various sizes, you can better display them by covering the sides of the box with clear adhesive-plastic before you cut it out. This will allow you to use tape to hold the pictures on the box without harming the box itself.

Teaching Pictures

These may be used not only to visualize unfamiliar items but also to bring out feelings and "what if" situations. Situation pictures can be used to set the tone for a lesson by asking questions, such as "What's going on here?" or "What would you do in this situation?" These kinds of pictures can help guide conversations, start discussions, and explore emotions. Collect these from magazines, calendars, newspapers, old Sunday-school lessons, etc.

Teaching Tree

By using a sturdy, dead tree branch you can make a tree for all seasons for your classroom. Plant your teaching tree in a small bucket and use plaster or crushed rock to keep it in place. You can spray paint the branch and/or the bucket if desired.

Use the tree as a room decoration and hang pictures or ornaments on it for different seasons. For example, you can use paper snowflakes for January, hearts for February, crosses for Easter, butterflies or flowers for spring, etc. The tree can also become an excellent display for items you want to emphasize from lessons. For example, hang on it memory verses, prayer reminders, pictures or names of Bible characters or missionaries, dates of children's birthdays, special events, etc.

Thumbodies

Everyone's fingerprints are different. Thumbodies make use of this unique quality as a teaching tool. Not only do thumbodies teach us how very special we are to God, but they can be fun as well. Let students make fingerprints with a stamp pad and paper. Most stamp pads now have washable ink, but be prepared for a mess anyway. Have paper towels handy and suggest students wash up after class. Provide smocks for students to wear during this activity. (See CRAFT SMOCKS.)

Let the children try their creativity and make figures out of these fingerprints by adding features or bodies. Some suggestions for guided discussion: you are thumbody special to God; you can tell thumbody about Jesus; bring thumbody to Sunday school, church, or VBS with you.

Thumbodies can also become a teaching tool by using them to illustrate flash cards for a review game. Use 3" x 5" index cards in assorted colors. Select significant events from Bible lessons you have studied and draw them on the index cards. Add thumbodies where the Bible person would be in the scene. Use your thumb for large figures and pointer finger for the others. Add clothing, weapons, and background as needed. On the back of the card list the occasion illustrated, where the story is found in the Bible, important people involved, and the reference for a key verse. Keep these mini flash cards in a card file or suitable box. Add an instruction card which can be glued in the lid of the box. Instructions can be as follows:

1. Work alone or with a friend.
2. Name the story.
3. Identify the Bible people in the story and tell what they did.
4. If you have questions, check the story reference for answers.
5. Say the key verse or look it up from the reference.

Children will enjoy these mini flash cards and can even make their own set to take home.

Time Lines

This is a good way to show chronological order for children who don't understand time by years or decades. You can illustrate events on a large piece of newsprint or poster board. For very young children, use clothespins to attach pictures to a piece of string or yarn. A lesson can be reviewed by having the children pin up the pictures in the correct order.

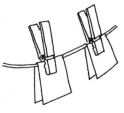

TV Envelope

This aid is developed for individual student use. Any size envelope will do. Cut out a "window" in the center front, seal the flap, and cut the ends of the envelope out. For the story strip use a long strip of paper wide enough to slip through the envelope easily. Draw or mount pictures on the story strip, leaving a section on either end of it blank. These blank sections provide a hand hold for pulling the pictures through the envelope. The student will pull the strip through the "window" and thus view the story. Be sure the window and picture size are the same so only one picture is viewed at a time.

TV Set

Use a medium-size cardboard box for this aid. Remove the top of the box. Cut out a section of one side the size of your "screen." Make matching holes at both sides of the top and bottom of the box for insertion of the dowel rollers. A strip of pictures will attach to these two dowels so that the pictures can be turned. The picture strip can be made of either recycled pictures or hand-drawn ones. Tape them together to form one long strip. Be sure the screen and picture size are the same so only one picture is viewed at a time.

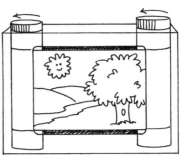

Vacation Pack

This makes a nice gift for vacationing students. Use a large manila envelope and include lesson material and take-home papers from the lessons that will be missed. Other items you may wish to add: games to play in the car or for rainy days (purchase inexpensive ones or make your own from reproducible books (See the book *Let the Games Begin!* by Standard Publishing for more information on making creative reproducible games for teaching Scripture.); a list of interesting places and Christian locales to see (camps, churches, and museums); helps for family devotions; puzzle books; Christian magazines; note paper, pencil, envelopes, and stamps. Include a personal note of remembrance to the student, assuring him/her of your love and prayers.

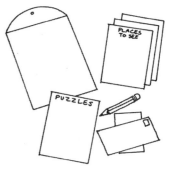

Video Cameras

Video camcorders are quite popular and can be used to tape classes, programs, VBS, etc. Everyone enjoys having this visual reminder of special times together. These videos also make good program material for an entire church or school by reviewing unique events in the family of God.

V.I.P. Frame

This is a frame that can be used to spotlight special papers your students have written or areas of study they have researched. The frame is for Very Important Papers by Very Important People. Draw a large head, hands and feet on construction paper. Color and cut these out. Glue them to the back of a 9" x 12" sheet of construction paper. Have students write on only one side of their paper. Staple any additional papers to the top edge of the first paper so you can raise them to read the information underneath it. Use double-sided or masking tape to attach the papers to the construction paper. Then you can change them without destroying the construction paper underneath.

Visualized Bible Verses

Combining descriptive pictures with construction paper words or phrases is an excellent way to teach memory verses. Prepare these as for flannelgraph figures. (See FLANNELGRAPH FIGURES). Use pictures that illustrate the words or phrases. Print the words or phrases on construction paper below or beside the pictures.

Visualized Songs

Well-loved songs can be visualized easily. If you make them in book form, they will stand up better under constant use. Use large sheets of lightweight poster board. Fold these in half and use one half of the page for the words and the other for your illustrations. Pictures can be drawn or cut from magazines or old Sunday school papers. If you use watercolor markers, you can print on both sides of your pages so each poster board piece will make four pages. A simple book can have holes punched in the pages and metal rings inserted.

A sturdier method is to bind the pages into a heavy cardboard cover. Cut a piece of corrugated cardboard 2" longer and 2" wider than the open sheet of poster board. Score and fold this cover piece in the middle. Cover the outside of the cover with a patterned adhesive-plastic. Make the plastic about 1" larger all around than the cardboard so you can fold it over the edges and to the inside. Now cut a piece of plastic slightly smaller than the cardboard and cover the inside surface. This piece should cover the tucked in edges of the outside piece. Staple the pages into the book on the fold. If you end up with an uneven number of pages, make a special last page. Fold one piece of poster board in half and cut it 1" longer than the fold. This will fit under the other pages and allow the page to be anchored when stapled.

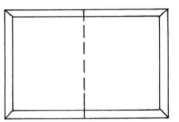

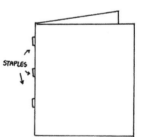

STAPLES

Water Play

Many of the Bible stories take place on or near a body of water. Examples are Jonah and the big fish, Jesus' calming the sea, the fishermen and Jesus, Paul's shipwreck, etc. While it is active fun, water play is also an excellent introduction to these stories. Cover a table with a towel or plastic tablecloth. Use a dishpan of water to illustrate the story.

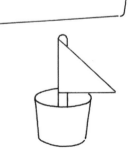

Paper or Styrofoam cups, cut-off milk cartons, or Styrofoam slabs make small boats. Cut the Styrofoam slabs into shapes for boats. Make a paper sail and glue it to a craft stick or tongue depressor mast. Stick this into the Styrofoam.

A larger boat, such as Noah's ark, can be made from the top of a fast-food carton and a Styrofoam meat tray. Glue the carton top inside the tray with waterproof glue. Draw a window on the carton with a permanent-ink marker. Glue pictures of animals and Noah and his family inside these window lines.

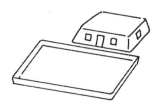

Chenille wire or clothespin figures could also be used for water play. (See section FIGURES.)

Whiteboard

Use sturdy cardboard and cover it with Con-Tact whiteboard plastic. This product (Rubbermaid Company) comes in rolls like other adhesive-plastic and can be used for doors, dividers, etc. Use <u>dry-erase</u> markers for writing and facial tissues or paper towels for erasing. Make a small board to stick inside your flannelboard for use on outings, camps, or VBS. You can make a chalkboard on the other side of the cardboard to provide a portable teaching center for your class. (See CHALKBOARD.)

Word Plays

These are easy to make and fun to complete. They provide another way of stressing your lesson aim or learning the memory verse and are good fillers when you need something extra to take up class time. Several basic methods are possible.

vowel omission
This technique leaves spaces where vowels would normally appear in words.
Example: J_S_S CHR_ST   (JESUS CHRIST)

consonant omission
In this method, spaces are substituted for consonants.
Example: _E_U_ _ _ _I_ _   (JESUS CHRIST)

scrambled words
All the letters of a word are present but in mixed-up order.
Example: SEJUS STICHR   (JESUS CHRIST)

reverse verse
This word play reverses the order of the letters, so all words are spelled backwards.
Example: SUSEJ TSIRHC   (JESUS CHRIST)

key letters
Here a number of letters are missing, but some of the key ones are given. This provides some help for students.
Example: J_ _ U_ _ _RI_ T   (JESUS CHRIST)

miss-spaced words

All the words are present in a sentence, but they are miss-spaced. Some break off in the middle of the word while others are added to the next word.

Example: JES USCHRIST ISTH ESO NOFG OD.

(JESUS CHRIST IS THE SON OF GOD.)

extra letters

Excess letters are inserted wherever desired just to add fun to teaching techniques.

Example: Remove all the X's to read. XJXXESXXXUXS CX-HXRXIXXXSXT (JESUS CHRIST)

Crafts

Aluminum Foil Covering

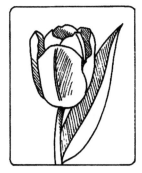

Foil can be used to cover a number of things, such as juice cans, Styrofoam meat trays, cardboard containers, or tin cans. By using string and this process, you can make the surfaces of these items look like fancy-design metallic objects.

Make a design, such as a flower or geometric figure, on the surface of your object by gluing string to it. Apply a coat of thick white glue over the area you want to cover with the foil. Crinkle the foil and then lay it over the surface. Press it down around the string design and close to all parts of the object you are covering. Allow glue to dry.

Spray black paint over the foil and wipe it off right away with a soft cloth. This spraying and wiping is what gives the foil its metallic look. Add a coat of clear craft glaze or spray to give the foil more sparkle.

You can use this same method to cover cardboard figures and make them look metallic. These figures can then be used either as sculptures or glued to plain backgrounds to make pictures.

Batik

This is a method of using fabric dyes and wax to decorate cotton cloth. Because hot wax burns, this is a project that needs adult supervision! Wash and iron the cotton cloth before decorating it.

Melt equal amounts of paraffin and beeswax in the top of a double boiler. Tape or tack a piece of cotton fabric on top of a thick layer of newspapers. Draw a simple pattern on the cloth with a pencil. Brush melted wax on all the sections of the design except the ones you want to dye. The wax needs to soak completely through the cloth.

Mix the dye following the package directions. Add a pinch of salt to the mixture. Soak the cloth in this dye solution until it is the color you desire. Rinse the fabric in cold water and blot it with newspapers. Hang it up to dry.

You can make a design in two shades of one color by brushing melted wax on any areas that you don't want to get a deeper color. Repeat the dyeing, rinsing, and drying steps. This process can be repeated as often as desired with the same color to get darker shades. Or you can apply a different color in the same manner.

After the design is completed, lay the fabric on a thick layer of newspapers. Place one newspaper on top of the cloth and press it with a hot iron to remove the wax from the fabric. If you have several layers of wax, you will need to change the newspaper often to enable it to absorb the wax. Never iron the cloth directly as it will cause the surface of the iron to become coated with wax.

crayon etching

Use bright-colored crayons to make thick patches of color on a sheet of paper. When you have covered the paper with these patches, color over the whole page with black crayon. Scratch a design on the black crayon using a sharp object, such as an unbent paper clip or a nail. The black color will come off and your picture will show up as brightly-colored lines and areas wherever you scratch the design. When you are done with the picture, polish it gently with a piece of paper towel.

crayon resist

A crayon resist is a technique that combines both crayons and paint. First a design is drawn on the paper with crayons. Use white or light-colored crayons for this. Put a concentrated layer of crayon on the design area. Lay the picture on a thick layer of newspapers or paper towels. Use a wide brush and paint a layer of thin dark tempera or acrylic paint over the entire page. The crayon will "resist" the paint and the design will show up as a white or light-colored picture.

Dough Art

Figures and ornaments made from dough are simple to make and lots of fun too. There are many kinds of these doughs.

Inedible doughs

baked dough
1/4-1/2 cup salt
1 cup flour
1/4-1/2 cup warm water
Mix flour, salt, and 1/4 cup of the water together slowly, stirring the mixture as you pour in the water. Add more water if needed until the dough is like pie dough. Form figures on aluminum foil, using the dough like clay. This same mixture of salt and flour can be scattered on the foil to keep dough from sticking to it.

Make figures about 1/2" thick as thin figures tend to bend when cooling. Use food coloring in small batches of the dough for color variations. You can add straw flowers, seeds, or pieces of wood for decorations or make textures with a fork or toothpick before the dough figures are baked. If you are going to hang the figures, place an unbent paper clip in them now. Push the clip until only about 1/4" sticks out. Bake the figures on a foil covered cookie sheet for 45-60 minutes at 300 degrees. The figures

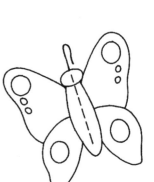

will make a hollow sound when tapped if they are done. Be sure to bake them long enough. Allow figures to cool on the foil-covered cookie sheet. Add paint decorations and shellac finish if desired.

bread dough
8 tablespoons white glue
8 slices stale white bread
2 teaspoons glycerine (from drugstore)
Cut off the crusts and discard them. Crumble the bread slices into a mixing bowl. Mix the glue and 1 teaspoon of the glycerine into the bread crumbs thoroughly. Coat your hands with the rest of the glycerine and knead the dough until pliable. Let the dough set overnight in a plastic bag.

coffee and cornmeal dough
1 1/2 cups cornmeal
warm water
2 cups used, dry coffee grounds
1/2 cup salt
Combine all dry ingredients and add enough warm water to moisten them.

cornmeal dough
1 1/2 cups cornmeal
1 cup salt
1 1/2 cups flour
1 cup water
Combine all ingredients and stir until they stick together. If needed, add more water. You can keep this dough for six weeks in an airtight container.

no-bake dough
2 cups flour
2 cups salt
1/2 cup hot water
1 teaspoon cooking oil
1 tablespoon powdered alum (from a drugstore)
Mix these ingredients together in a bowl. If the dough is too dry, add more water. Divide the dough into small amounts and add food coloring to get different colors. Work on wax paper and mold the dough into desired shapes. Roll it into coils or cut it with cookie cutters and mark designs with a toothpick. Allow the figures to dry for several days or aid drying by baking them for about three hours in a 250 degree oven. Leftover dough keeps well in a plastic bag in the refrigerator. The alum will keep the dough from spoiling.

vinegar dough

1 cup salt

1 cup water

3 cups flour

1/4 cup cooking oil

2 tablespoons vinegar

Mix ingredients together, stirring well. If necessary, add more water to obtain correct consistency. Knead the dough. Place unused dough in a plastic zipper-bag. It will keep in the refrigerator indefinitely. If the dough starts to dry out, moisten it periodically and knead in a bit more water.

Edible Doughs

All these doughs should be used and eaten the same day they are made.

brown sugar n' peanut butter dough

1/4 cup brown sugar

1/4 cup peanut butter

1 tablespoon granola

Mix all ingredients together. If the mixture is too dry, add more peanut butter. If it is too sticky, add more brown sugar.

cookie and cake dough

1 pound of powdered sugar

1/3 C light corn syrup

1/3 C melted butter or margarine

1/2 tsp. salt

1 tsp vanilla

paste food coloring

By hand, mix together corn syrup, butter, salt, and vanilla. Add sugar and knead until smooth. If the mixture is sticky, add more sugar until the dough becomes pliable. Divide it into small batches and color these with food coloring. For a very special occasion, decorate cookies or cupcakes with this dough. You can refrigerate unused dough in a plastic bag for up to two weeks. Warm it to room temperature before reusing.

frosting dough

 1/2 cups powdered sugar

1 cup peanut butter

1 can frosting mix

Mix and knead all ingredients until the dough is pliable.

honey and peanut butter dough

2 cups powdered milk

1 cup honey
1 cup peanut butter
Mix and knead all ingredients together. If necessary, add more powdered milk.

spice dough
2 teaspoons baking powder
2 cups flour
1/3 cup sugar
1/2 teaspoon cinnamon
1/2 teaspoon salt
1/2 teaspoon nutmeg
1/3 cup milk
4 tablespoons cooking oil
Combine dry ingredients. Add oil and milk to this mixture and knead until it is the consistency of pie dough. After rolling or shaping, fry it in oil at 375 degrees.

Finger Paint

All finger paints are used just as their name indicates — with the fingers. They are generally used on the glossy side of paper, such as shelf or butcher paper which has been dipped in water. Shelf paper works well for class murals as it provides a continuous roll. Finger painting is great fun not only for young children but all ages as it supplies tactile learning and experience with different kinds of textures. You don't have to confine its use to art either. Have students write memory verses or the answers to review questions in the paint. Be sure to cover table surfaces with plastic or newspapers and have students use craft smocks!

edible finger paint
Young children seem to have to stick everything in their mouths — including paint. You can make several types of edible finger paint.

1. Add food coloring to small amounts of Cool Whip or other dessert topping. You can also use the aerosol cans of topping. Just spray directly onto the paper and add the food coloring. Let students mix the color in as they paint.

2. Use instant pudding mix. Mix as directed. Add food coloring to vanilla to obtain a variety of colors. For more student participation, put the pudding mix and milk into a jar. Cover it tightly and let the students shake it until the mix is thickened.

3. Sprinkle 2-3 teaspoons of flavored gelatin mix over the wet sheet of paper. The darker colors such as black cherry, grape, cherry, and strawberry are not only colorful, but give off a wonderful fragrance. This recipe is great fun in textures because it is grainy, then slippery, then sticky, and finally grainy again when dry.

4. Spread canned frosting mix onto the paper and use as finger paint.

regular finger paint

There are a large number of recipes for finger paints.

1 cup liquid starch
water
2 cups powdered tempera paint
Mix the starch and tempera until smooth. Slowly add just enough water to make the mixture nice and smooth.

4 tablespoons liquid starch
water
1 cup powdered tempera paint
2 teaspoons liquid dish soap
Mix starch, paint, and soap. Carefully stir in only enough water to make mixture smooth.

1 cup wheat paste
water
3 tablespoons powdered tempera paint
1 tablespoon Ivory soap flakes (optional)
Mix the paste and tempera, adding enough water to make mixture smooth. If desired, you can add the soap flakes to make the paint smoother.

2 tablespoons liquid dish soap
3 cups flour
3/4 cup water
powdered tempera paint or food coloring
Mix together soap, flour, and water until the consistency is that of a thick paste. Color with tempera or food coloring.

1 cup powdered soap
1/4 cup water
5 tablespoons liquid tempera paint
Mix together soap and paint. Add enough water to make mixture smooth.

Flour Fun

By combining flour and water in different amounts you can come up with some inexpensive paints and paste. In each case, add water slowly so you don't change the consistency of your mixture.

1. A small amount of water in flour makes a sticky, paste-like mixture.

2. Mix a larger amount of water into the flour until the mixture is smooth and thick and you have finger paint.

3. Mix still more water into the flour and stir until smooth and you can use it for painting with a brush.

By adding a drop or two of food coloring you can tint the paste or paint. Here again, be careful, as too much color can change the consistency of the mixture!

Glue Ornaments

Thick white craft glue makes a delicate and unusual ornament to hang in a window as a suncatcher or on a Christmas tree. Select a simple pattern for your ornament. Limit the size to about 2″ in diameter as these ornaments may curl when hung. Lay a piece of transparent plastic wrap over the pattern on a flat surface and tape the wrap down so there are no wrinkles.

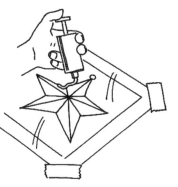

Trace over this pattern on the plastic wrap with the glue. A small hand applicator that has a plunger and small nozzle makes this much easier to do. These are usually available at a craft store. Start at the bottom of your design and push away from yourself. This enables you to see the glue as it emerges. Keep just ahead of this glue line. Do curves in a continuous line, but stop and start new lines where there are sharp angles. Go back and fill in broken lines after you have done the original pattern.

While the glue is still wet, sprinkle the ornament with glitter or add beads, sequins, or tiny pom-poms for trims. Let the designs set for 24 hours before turning them over to dry on the other side. Then allow about another day for them to dry completely. If you don't use glitter or other metallic materials, they can be quick-dried in a microwave oven for about 10 minutes or until they turn clear in color.

If you make a mistake while tracing the pattern, scrape the glue off and wipe the plastic wrap with a damp cloth. Then start over.

Leather-look Paper

Dissolve a package of fabric dye in a pan of hot water. Crumple up some shelf paper and boil it in the dye mixture for 5 minutes. Rinse the paper in cold water and squeeze the water out of it carefully. Spread the paper out to dry. This will add variety to your bulletin board or teaching figures!

Maché

Machés can be made of various materials. They are used to make sculptures, pinatas, jewelry, plaques, etc. Some machés need a form to wrap around, while others are molded with the hands like clay.

papier maché

All papier machés have two common ingredients — paper and paste. These two materials can be varied in many ways. Machés are also made in similar ways. They use either strips or small pieces of the paper which are then added in some manner to the paste. Here are some basic recipes:

Tear strips of paper. You can use newspaper, tissue paper, newsprint, or paper towels for this. Mix wallpaper or wheat paste with warm water until it is a smooth paste. You can make your own paste instead of using wallpaper or wheat paste. Simply cook 1 part cornstarch and 8 parts of water in a double boiler until it is as thick as pudding.

After cooling, it can be used as paste in any recipe for papier mache. White glue or liquid laundry starch can also be substituted instead of the wallpaper or wheat paste.

You will need some sort of a mold, like a balloon, cardboard, or aluminum foil figure to wrap the mache' around. Dip the paper strips into the paste and wrap them around the base. Completely cover the base by overlapping the strips and using several layers of them. Use your hands to wipe off any extra paste and smooth the figure. Allow it to dry thoroughly on wax paper. It will air dry very hard. You can paint and decorate it as desired after drying. You may want to add 1-2 coats of a gesso, white base paint, or shellac before you paint it.

A finer mixture which can be used like clay for items like plaques, jewelry, maps, etc., can be made by mixing tiny pieces of paper towel, crepe paper, or newspaper with a wheat paste. Let the mixture stand overnight then squeeze out the liquid. Mold it over a base, press it into a greased cookie mold, or roll it out on wax paper and use a knife to cut desired shapes. Let items dry thoroughly. You can speed the drying of the cut shapes by baking them in a 200 degree oven until they are dry. Paint and shellac finished items.

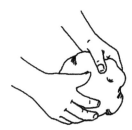

crepe papier maché

    1 cup flour
    1/2 cup salt
    3 1/2 cups crepe paper
    few drops of vanilla extract

Tear the crepe paper into strips and soak them in water. Squeeze out the water and add the flour, salt, and vanilla. The latter offsets the disagreeable smell. Knead the mixture into a moldable dough. WARNING: colored crepe paper stains hands, so wear rubber or plastic gloves. You can paint objects made of white crepe paper when they are dry.

tissue papier maché

    facial or bathroom tissue

white glue
liquid starch

Tear the tissues into strips and soak them in the starch until they are pulpy. Add some of the white glue to enable this mush to hold its shape when dry. Mold the pulp into a ball and squeeze out as much starch as possible. You can make colored objects by using colored tissue. If desired, you can paint items that are made from white tissue when completely dry.

cotton ball maché

1 bag small cotton balls
1 cup flour
3/4 to 1 cup water

Make a thick, smooth paste by mixing the flour and water together. Dip the cotton balls, one at a time, into this mixture. Gently remove each ball, letting extra paste drip off. The balls puff up in the paste and will stay that way with careful handling. Mold the balls together into shapes on a foil-covered or no-stick cookie sheet. Bake for about an hour in a 325 degree oven until the items are light brown and hard. You can paint these items when cool if desired.

sand maché

1 cup wallpaper paste
water
6 cups sand

Mix the sand and paste together. Add enough water to make the sand feel sticky and pack together like clay. The finer the sand used, the smoother the surface will be. This will take about two days' drying time. You can smooth the surface with sandpaper if desired. This is a great outdoor craft for making permanent sand buildings using different containers and adding details with nature items such as shells and twigs. You can make your own Bible-times village, Nehemiah's walls of Jerusalem, or Queen Esther's palace.

sawdust maché

1 cup wheat or wallpaper paste
2 cups sawdust
1/2 cup water

Strain sawdust to remove any splinters. Mix the ingredients, adding only enough water to make the maché moldable.

soap maché

1 cup Ivory soap flakes
1/4 cup water

Add 1/8 cup of water to the soap flakes and beat with an egg-beater until the mixture is flaky. If necessary, add more water. This maché takes a long time to dry but makes nice figures for pretty guest soaps for the bathroom. It may help to harden objects by placing them in the refrigerator.

Metallic-look Paper Figures

Plain brown grocery bags can be used to make 3-dimensional paper craft that looks like metal. Select a simple pattern for your figure or picture. You can add separate arms, legs, wings, etc. Cut two layers of the bag from your pattern. Between these sections, lay a piece of 22 gauge floral wire wherever you will want to bend and shape the figure. Glue the wire and paper together with white glue. Shape the figure while it is still wet. Allow to dry.

Brush both sides of each piece of the figure with a heavy coat of thick white glue, such as Tacky. Burn this coating until each piece is completely blackened by rotating the pieces over a candle flame immediately after applying the glue. Let pieces dry overnight. When they are dry, rub them with a soft cloth. This cleans off the sooty residue and makes the figure look metallic. To add to this look, rub a little gold wax or paint (available in craft stores) over the pieces. Assemble the figure and use it free-standing or mount it on a background to make a 3-D picture.

Newspaper Crafts

Old newspaper can be used to make lightweight items for mobiles or inexpensive jewelry. Glue 3 or 4 thicknesses of newspaper together with white glue. Use a simple pattern to trace a shape on this wet, layered newspaper. Cut out the shape and punch a hole in the top of it with a darning needle, so it can be strung later. Add details to the figure using a blunt pencil, toothpick, or table knife. You can curve the shape up or down by laying it across a curved object while it is drying. This allows you to curve wings for butterflies, birds, etc. Let the newspaper figure set for 12-24 hours until completely dry. Paint the figure with acrylic hobby paints. Small details, such as eyes or fine lines, can be done by dipping toothpicks into the paint and tracing or dotting it on the figure. If you desire a harder finish and have older students you can use enamel model paint instead of the acrylics. These figures can be used for jewelry by gluing them to appropriate backing pieces, such as pin or barrette bases.

Paint

egg-yolk paint
Beat 1 teaspoon water and 1 teaspoon of sugar into 3 egg yolks.

Pour this mixture into several small containers, such as jar lids. Add a drop or two of food coloring. Paint designs on cookies or other objects with small paintbrushes. When dry, this paint makes a bright, shiny design.

glue paint

Regular white glue can be mixed with food coloring to make a glue paint. This kind of paint can be used on paper, wood, plastic, fabric, glass, metal, pasta, and glue dough.

For a special marble effect, paint the surface of item with a base coat of glue-paint and add drops of a second color while the first is still wet. Swirl this second color around with a toothpick or straw to get a marbled look.

soap paint

Use an egg beater to whip Ivory soap flakes and water together in a bowl until the mixture is the consistency of stiff egg whites. Equal amounts of soap and water should be used. Add food coloring to water before beating to get different colors. Soap paint can be used for fingerpainting. Let the picture dry overnight before you move it. You can also use a brush to paint this mixture on a washable surface, such as a plastic tablecloth, Styrofoam tray, or the sidewalk.

For different looks in painting, try one or more of the following techniques:

1. To add an extra "sparkle" to a picture, add glitter while the paint is still wet.

2. Paint with a toothbrush. You can spatter the paint over the surface of the paper by holding the brush side toward the paper and rubbing your finger over the brush.

3. Mix paint with water to thin it. Drop several paint globules on your paper then use a straw to blow them around.

4. Dip irregular-shaped sponge pieces into tempera paint and use them instead of brushes.

5. Use cotton swabs, craft sticks, feathers, fingers and/or toes, or craft sticks instead of brushes.

6. Let students make patterns by running a toy car, rolling marbles, or pulling strings through it.

7. Try different textures by mixing sawdust, coffee grounds, or salt to the paint or sprinkling them on wet paint surfaces.

Paper Weaving

There are several different ways you can weave paper, but they are all based on the same method. You will need two colors of construction paper. Fold one piece in half lengthwise. Cut slits in this paper, beginning at the fold, and cutting to within about 1" from

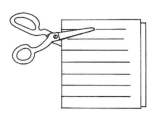

the edge. For straight line weaving, cut these slits evenly spaced across the paper. Unfold the paper. Cut the other piece of paper into strips. You will use these strips for weaving. Take one strip and go over the first slit, under the next one, over the one after that, etc. Continue in this manner alternating the over and under technique the length of your base paper. The second strip starts just the opposite—under the first slit, over the next one, under the one after that. Weave strips until your base paper is full. Tape or glue the ends of each strip down so it can't move out of place. Just for fun try some of these variations:

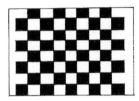

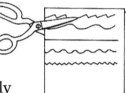

1. Cut wavy, curly, or zig-zag strips in the base paper instead of straight, evenly-spaced ones.

2. Cut the weaving strips into different widths. Vary these widths as you weave.

3. Use more than 1 color weaving strips.

Pasta Decorations

Pasta, such as macaroni, is often used for craft projects. Usually the macaroni is glued to the project and then painted. Why not try using colored pasta instead? Place the pasta, along with some food coloring and a small amount of alcohol, in a jar and shake it until it is colored evenly. Spread the pasta out on a piece of paper toweling and allow it to dry before using.

Rice Decorations

Colored, uncooked rice can be used for craft projects. Place the rice and some food coloring in a jar and shake until the rice is evenly colored. Spread the rice out on paper toweling and allow it to dry before using.

Rubber Stamps

Rubber stamps can be a lot of fun for crafts. Take one simple image and try out some of these variations:

1. Create a background by stamping the picture all over the paper to fill in the page.

2. Stamp the image around the paper sides to create borders.

3. Use only part of the stamp by allowing only the segment you want to touch the paper.

4. Move or slide the stamp across the paper to create a sense of motion. This will blur the lines and make it look like the image is moving. Or you can also add "action" lines by drawing them in. Yet another way to get movement is by stamping the picture several times without re-inking. In this way the image fades into the distance.

5. Use watercolor markers to paint the stamp instead of a stamp pad.

6. After you have used the above method and stamped the image, use a damp cotton swab and brush some of the color around to give it a watercolor appearance.

7. Use colored pencils or fine tip markers to color the picture after it has been stamped.

8. Glue sequins, beads, flowers, etc. on the image or paper to add details or backgrounds.

9. Make several identical images on different pieces of paper. Cut them out and glue them on top of one another with white glue to create a 3-D look. Color or decorate one of these pictures and use it as the top piece. You can add small pieces of cardboard or Styrofoam to build up different heights between layers. These ornaments can be used for mobiles or additions to other craft items, such as boxes and pictures. They can even become jewelry, such as pins or necklaces, by gluing them to appropriate backing pieces or threading them on yarn or monofilament.

10. Make fold-over cards by stamping the picture near the bottom edge of the paper. Cut along the bottom half of the image and trim outward on both sides of it to the sides of the paper. Fold this cut side down over the rest of the page and write your message inside. Add an outside greeting if you desire.

Keep your stamps clean to insure sharp, true-color pictures. When you are finished using it, clean the stamp thoroughly with liquid dish soap or window cleaner and a toothbrush. Keep the wood and mounting glue dry. Blot dry the stamp with a lint-free cloth or quality paper towel. Store it out of heat, direct sunlight, or dust.

Sand Pictures

Colored sand can be used to make layered sand pictures. Dye the sand by placing white sand and food coloring in a jar. Shake the sand until it is all evenly dyed. Spread it out on paper toweling and allow it to dry before using. Use a small jar, such as a baby-food jar, to make a sand picture. Add layers of colored sand and create your own design by varying the thickness of these layers.

Shrinky-Dinks

Use pieces of plastic glasses or the clear plastic lids, such as those that come on containers of meat or salad, to make your own shrinky-dinks. Draw a design on the plastic and color it in with permanent-ink markers. Cut out the figure and lay it on a cookie sheet. Place it in an oven at 350 degrees for a few minutes until it shrinks.

Starch Stuff

Liquid starch can offer craft variations for students.

hangings

Coat a sheet of wax paper with liquid starch using a brush or your hand. Make a design on this paper with flat items, such as silk flowers, real flowers and leaves, pieces of cloth, yarn, or gift wrap. Lay another sheet of wax paper over the top and press the layers together. Allow the hanging to dry overnight. Use a paper punch to make a hole at one end of it. Thread yarn, monofilament, or thread through this hole and hang your creation in a window. By adding a squirt or two of white glue to the starch, you can cut drying time.

balloon molds

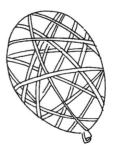

This is a good activity to do with a partner. Blow up a balloon and tie it. One student can hold this balloon while the other works on it. Cover the entire balloon with a thin layer of petroleum jelly. Immerse pieces of yarn into a container of liquid starch and intertwine these pieces around the balloon so as to create a mesh effect. Allow the yarn-wrapped balloon to dry completely on a piece of wax paper. Pop the balloon and remove the pieces from the mesh. You can vary the shapes of the creations by using balloons of different sizes and shapes.

Hints and

Shortcuts

Adding Machine Tape

Rolls of adding machine tape are handy to have for teaching aids and crafts. Use them in TV Envelopes and for making cartoon strips or mini-murals.

Adhesive Plastic

When using adhesive plastic to cover several small pieces for a game, simply draw or glue all of them on cardboard first. Cover and then cut apart. This saves time and makes handling them easier.

Use patterned plastic to cover storage boxes and the covers of visualized songs. Protect aids, such as games, books, finger puppets, etc. with clear plastic.

Hair spray removes permanent ink from plastic-coated or laminated materials. Keep a travel or sample size of spray handy in the classroom.

A light rubbing with cold cream will keep plastic-coated or laminated materials in good condition. Treat them with this once a year. Be sure to wipe all excess cold cream off, so markers will work.

To make Color and Wipe books for younger children, use reproducible patterns that have simple line drawings. Make enough pages for a book. Bind the pages together with metal notebook rings. Cover all pages with clear adhesive plastic and provide students with wipe-off crayons or watercolor markers. The pictures can be colored, then the pages cleaned for reuse.

Use scraps of clear adhesive plastic to make suncatchers or bookmarks. Place pressed flowers, leaves, or even butterflies between two scraps of the plastic. Cut the suncatcher into a geometric shape. Thread a length of black thread or monofilament (like fishing line) through it and hang it on a suction hook in a window. Cut the plastic into a long rectangle for a bookmark. By using pinking or scalloping shears, you can add an interesting border.

Art Projects

Plan ahead when you are deciding on an art project for your class. Think about the results as well as the materials you need. Consider, "What's the worst thing that could happen?" Prepare for that eventuality as much as you can. Make allowance for the clean-up period as well as any possible accidents.

Always make up a sample to show students the finished product. This enables you to try out all the directions ahead of class and change or clarify instructions. The sample also serves as a motivator to complete the project.

If you are working with modeling clay and don't plan to dry it in an oven, use a little bit of white glue for every handful of clay. This helps prevent the object from breaking when it is dry.

By adding a few tablespoons of vegetable oil to modeling clay, you can make it easier to handle.

To prevent play doughs and maché clays from getting moldy, add 1-2 tablespoons of powdered alum to them.

A few drops of oil of peppermint, perfume, or bath oil, will not only keep clay mixes from spoiling, but will help them to stay sweet smelling as well.

To preserve chalk drawings for a long time, spray them with evaporated milk or hair spray.

A few drops of liquid soap added to tempera paint will allow the paint to adhere to aluminum foil or tin cans.

If the edges of a sheet of finger painting curl up, turn the dry painting over and gently press it with a warm iron.

By adding liquid soap to finger paints, you help prevent staining and make clothes washing easier.

Always add powdered or paste coloring to dry ingredients for finger paints. Liquid colors should be added to water. Otherwise the colors are harder to mix in and may cause variations in mixture consistency.

Use pinking shears or scalloping scissors to make decorative edges on art projects made of wax paper or clear adhesive plastic.

You can make your own soap flakes for craft recipes by grating a bar of Ivory soap on a kitchen grater.

Substitute cotton swabs for brushes when using paint with water books with young children. The cotton swabs are much easier to handle.

Awards

Use the free paper crowns from local restaurants to reward students for various classroom accomplishments. Blank out the restaurant's name and glue or tape a desired caption, such as "Memory" or "Attendance." (There are five books of **Award Certificates** available from Standard in reproducible form that can also be used for memory work, attendance, and special achievements.)

Bible Reading

When wanting several Bible passages read in class, write the references on slips of paper and place them in an envelope. Pass the envelope around the class and let those who are willing to read draw a slip out. This eliminates pressure for reluctant students. The method works especially well with adults.

Bulletin Boards

Always be on the lookout for ideas. Carry a small note pad or a few 3" x 5" index cards along, so you can make sketches and take notes when you visit other churches. Don't discount public school bulletin boards either. Many times you can adapt and adopt these basic ideas to Christian education.

Why not have a "show and tell" time when teachers can get together and share ideas about bulletin boards? Each person could bring an idea he/she has used. You can have several meetings and choose a specific Bible person, historical period, or topic to be featured at each one. Along this same line, you can have a "swap" time. When teachers feel they have used bulletin board visuals and lettering too often, let them "swap" with other teachers or place the items in the resource center for recycling.

Browse through teacher's lesson helps, magazines, or coloring books for ideas. Stroll through your local Christian bookstore and look at posters, greeting cards, or book jackets for more inspiration.

Try using or recycling cloth, felt, burlap, aluminum foil, or wallpaper as bulletin board backing. If taken care of properly, they can be used again and again.

Bulletin boards take a long time to make. Cover all your visuals with clear adhesive plastic so your work isn't wasted. That way they can be reused year after year.

Letters, visuals, and borders should be all ready to put up before you get to class. Place each word or phrase in a recycled envelope for easier handling.

Save yourself time by joining all the letters of a word instead of cutting out individual letters. Use stencils and overlap the letters slightly. Outline the entire word with a broad black outline before cutting it. This outline will help the words stand out for easier reading.

Keep the number of colors and visuals used at one time to a minimum. Remember—ONE idea to a board! It's better to have one or two large visuals than a number of small ones.

Place your board at student eye level.

Make lettering easy to read. Unless you are doing an acrostic, go across rather than up and down.

Recycle small plastic containers for storing letters. Mark the size and color on the lid. For example: 1" blue. You can separate and store letters in small groups, such as A-B-C in one container and D-E-F in another. Plastic zip bags also work well for storage.

Sometimes office or teacher's supply stores have bulletin board boarders on sale. These are usually corrugated or patterned and are good buys as they are reusable.

For neater corners on borders, fold the two adjoining sides into a mitered corner.

Cardboard

To make folding cardboard easier, score it first by laying a ruler along the line you want to fold. Use the point of a scissor to "draw" along this line. Be careful not to push so hard you cut completely through the cardboard. Always score cardboard on the outside surface at the place you are going to bend it.

When you use scissors to cut cardboard, you damage the edge of the cardboard. Use a knife and ruler to get a cleaner cut. Go over the cutting line several times until the cardboard breaks apart.

Cardboard Tubes

Paper towel tubes are good storage for maps, flags, pictures or extension cords. Simply roll them up and stick them through the cardboard tube.

Cassette Tapes

Use plastic shoe boxes to store cassette tapes neatly.

Chalkboards

Light adhesive drawer liner (Rubbermaid) can be used to make visual aids or decorations for chalkboards. This material sticks to the board and yet can be removed easily without harming the writing surface. The liner comes in patterns, colors, or plain white. Use permanent-ink markers to add details or to color white visuals before sticking them to the chalkboard.

Clothespins

Use spring-clip clothespins to keep children quiet during class. Clip a clothespin to each student's clothing. If the child becomes noisy, the clothespin is removed without comment by the teacher. If he stays quiet and keeps his clothespin, then he is rewarded.

To prevent papers from getting mixed up or students' playing with them during teaching time, print each student's name on a spring-clip clothespin. Make a few extra pins marked "Visitor." String a length of yarn or rope across one end of the room and place the clips on this line. Place it low enough for the students to reach it easily. Clip each child's craft items and any take-home materials with his/her pin as they are accumulated. At the end of class children can get their own items without help.

Copiers

There is a colored construction paper designed for use with copiers. Art Kraft by Bemiss-Jason has a smooth, shiny side which works well in copiers for reproducing patterns for craft projects.

Sometimes material you want to reproduce in a copier is printed on both sides of the paper. To avoid having the wrong side show through, lay a sheet of dark colored or black paper on the back side of the page you want to copy. Be sure this dark sheet is no larger than the material you want copied so you avoid any dark borders on your page.

Copying Patterns

To copy without using carbon paper, lay a thick layer of newspapers on the table. Place a sheet of typing paper on the newspaper. Lay the pattern you want to copy on top of this paper. Draw over the pattern using firm pressure. This will leave an impression on the typing paper. The pattern can then be drawn in with a pencil or marker.

Dental Floss

Use waxed dental floss to sew on items that receive hard use, such as metal buttons on costumes, movable parts on toys, or tactile pieces in busy books.

Directions

Sometimes when we give directions for an activity, we find that students are confused or the result is not what we expected. We need to have things clear in our own minds before we can help our students. Here are some things to think about as you prepare to give directions:

1. Set a goal or aim for the finished result.

2. Make up a sample or have a picture of the finished product. If it is a craft project with several steps, perhaps you need several samples to show each development.

3. Take into consideration the slow student as well as the whiz kid. Plan alternatives or extra helps for both.

4. Use visual aids to help you explain the various steps. These can be done on a chalkboard, large sheet of paper, or a page of directions given to each student.

5. Explain the activity from beginning to end before starting it. This will let your students proceed at their own speed.

6. Don't rush students. If the activity is too long for one period, extend it to two. This will eliminate stress and dissatisfied students.

7. Be able to answer the "why" of directions as well as the "how."

Be flexible. Maybe your students can find a better way of obtaining the same result than what you thought of. Don't take it as a personal attack on you if they do. God has given each person special gifts, and your students may be more creative than you expected.

Display Space

Short on shelves or tables? Use a fishnet hung from the lights, windows or pipes in your room. Use unbent paper clips for hangers to display your memory verses, pictures, or questions.

File Folders

Besides using folders for games, you can recycle them for filing use by:
1. Turning them inside out
2. Changing tab labels
3. Labeling them in pencil so they can be erased
Use colored folders to color code materials. File similar kinds of information in folders of the same color. An example is to file everything pertaining to prayer in blue folders, crafts in red, etc. An inexpensive variation of this is to use regular folders, but mark all similar files in the same color with a marker or colored label.

Finger Painting

Use freezer or butcher paper for finger painting rather than "finger paint" paper. You need a paper that is shiny and smooth on one side, but freezer and butcher paper are much less expensive than the other paper.

Flannelboards

Use your flannelboards for more than telling stories. You can use them to play games, such as tic-tac-toe by using yarn to make the game pattern. Flannelboards are also good places to display object lesson pictures, lesson outlines, or review questions.

Be sure to tilt a flannelboard or magnetic board out at the bottom in order to get the best results.

For variety use brushed nylon or fleece in bright colors for flannelboards.

Make sure the flannelboard is the right one for your specific story. It should be a size that can be easily seen and where figures aren't out of proportion when placed on it. If you are not using a background scene, check to see how your visuals look on the board itself. Some figures show best on a light background while others look better on a dark one.

Try covering your flannelboard with a piece of clear plastic tablecloth to protect your figures and background on rainy days as you enter or leave church. Cut the plastic slightly larger than your board.

Use an old roll-up window shade for a flannelboard. Glue or tape flannel to the front of the shade. Hang the shade on a wall and roll it down to use the flannelboard. When you are not using it, roll the shade up to get it out of your way.

Flannelgraph Figures

Use small pieces of velcro (hook side) for flannelgraph figures or removable costume pieces for puppets. Velcro will hold heavy objects that regular flannel backing won't or where extra sticking power is needed. This makes it ideal to use if you are going to present a flannelgraph outside where the wind can blow the pieces away. One word of caution: if you are using a flannelgraph where the flannel is glued to the board, velcro may tend to pull the flannel off. If the board is one that is inserted into a flannel covering, a small amount of velcro shouldn't hurt it.

Use old flannel sheets, shirts, and nightgowns as backing pieces for flannelgraph figures.

When you place a figure on the flannelboard, gently smooth it on in a sweeping motion from top to bottom. This enables it to have maximum adherence. Practice so the motion isn't distracting. Don't panic if a figure falls off the board. Children love to help you pick it up, and if you keep your composure, you can continue with a small "thank you" to your helper.

Place figures on your board at correct distances. Large ones go to the front, smaller ones to the back. Don't wave a figure around by the head while you talk about it! Place figures of people in normal positions. Be careful not to position them as though they are ready to fall off a chair or land on their noses.

Make sure all visuals are in the proper order. Many times if you get confused as to what happens next in your story a quick glance at the next visual will act as a prompter. If you use one figure several times in the story, lay it to one side, so you can find it again quickly.

Always stand at one side of your board, so students can see easily. If you are using a number of background scenes, clip them to the top of your board, so they can be flipped into place as needed.

Flash-Card Stories

Teachers who find it hard to manage flannelgraph figures may find it easier to mount the figures on construction paper backgrounds and use them as flash cards. Use only one side of each sheet of paper. Arrange the figures in scenes. Where a figure is used more than one place in the story, mount it individually and refer back to it when needed. Place a small tab on the bottom or one side of this page, so you can quickly flip back to it.

Mount a copy of the story on the backs of the flash cards. As you tell the story, move the pages shown to the back of those left in your hand. Glue each individual section to the back of the card just previous to it. In this way you can see or read it and use it for a prompter while displaying the picture that it describes. As some pictures in a story might be shown vertically while others are shown horizontally, glue the prompter section in the same direction as the picture which it describes. This will remind you which direction to hold the picture.

Games

Save the paper backing off adhesive plastic and use it to protect your table when gluing and coloring playing pieces.

For quick pockets for games, seal an envelope and then cut it in half. You will get two pockets from each envelope.

Use a penny instead of a die or spinner to determine moves for games. Heads mean you move two spaces and tails mean one space.

Try using a cube of urethane foam (used for upholstery) for game dice. They can be marked with a permanent ink marker and are much quieter to use than hard plastic dice.

Use self-sticking color coding 3/4" circles to make quick paths for playing pieces on game boards. You can print instructions on them if you wish.

Store small board or file folder games in 9" x 12" catalog envelopes. This provides protection for the game as well as keeping pieces together. Place the instructions on the front of the board or storage envelope. Game pieces can be placed in a small envelope or plastic zip bag and dropped inside or attached on the back.

Plastic zip bags are great for storage of playing pieces. To reinforce them for hanging, use a small square of plastic tape on both sides of one corner. Punch a hole through the reinforced corner and hang the bag or attach it to a game board with a small metal ring.

Gift Wrap

This versatile paper comes in a variety of patterns and colors. Use it to make borders and letters for bulletin boards. That way your lettering and border can match.

Gift wrap also makes storage envelopes for games more attractive. Cut the gift wrap slightly smaller than the size of the envelope. Glue it to the front of the envelope and mount the directions over this colorful background.

Ideas

Being creative is often not as much a matter of inborn talent as it is of being observant. Always be on the lookout for new ideas and adapt and adopt them to your specific needs. The following are some good ways to gather and store ideas.

1. Use a looseleaf notebook to keep track of ideas. When you see an idea for a craft project, activity, or teaching tip in a magazine, cut it out. Punch holes in it or glue it to a sheet of notebook paper and place it in the notebook. Do the same for notes you take at meetings, handouts you receive from seminars, or sketches you make while visiting other churches or schools.

2. When you have tried a new idea or project, jot down the results. List particulars, such as the class size, situation, problems encountered, successes achieved, or things you would change the next time.

3. Check out activity books or craft ideas in bookstores, supermarkets and discount stores, craft stores, or office supply stores. The latter is a good place to find new products that can be adapted to teaching and classroom use.

Label Maker

Use a label maker to make bracelets of memory verses or short notes of encouragement. Tape the ends together to form a bracelet. Children love to wear these and will remember the messages longer than if you write them on paper.

Library

Beginning or enlarging a library can be a problem if you are short of funds. Here are some tips that may help:

1. Have a special library emphasis month. Ask people to donate duplicate books or some they want to discard. Families can check on leftover books from their grown children.

2. Be on the lookout for books at flea markets, yard sales, or resale organizations, such as the Salvation Army or Goodwill. Many times these books can be bought for as little as 10-25 cents apiece.

3. Have a library gift tree at Christmas. Ask people to buy a book for the library and place it below a small artificial tree. Or print the name and a short description of various books you would like to add to the library on slips of paper. Tie the slips on the tree with bright-colored yarn and ask people to select a book to give to the library. Be sure to include the price of the book, so people know beforehand how much they will have to pay.

Sets of library books can quickly get out of place if several students or classes use them. Line up the books in correct order, left to right, and position a piece of colored plastic tape from the top of the first volume to the bottom of the last one. Carefully cut the tape between each volume and smooth the tape edges down. You can see at a glance if a book is out of order or missing.

Maps

When you have maps or charts that are used frequently, such as those of Paul's journeys, cover them with clear adhesive plastic. To help locate them easily, store them with bulletin board items. When your teaching pack has included good maps, preserve and recycle them in the same manner.

By turning a large wall map face side to the wall, you have a good screen for an overhead or slide projector.

You can make a good Bible geography game by taping a piece of clear plastic over a map and writing numbers by the important places. Students can come up and write a person's name, the place, or the event that happened there on the plastic with a watercolor marker or grease pencil.

Provide students with sheets of clear plastic large enough to cover a map in their Bibles or workbooks. By placing the plastic over the map, they can make personal notes with markers, grease pencils, or crayons to help them remember places or events they are currently studying. The plastic can be cleaned off and reused several times.

When you store maps, keep them in the order you will be using them throughout the year.

Markers

Use watercolor markers and washable paints whenever you can.

Not all markers labeled as "washable" will wash out completely from some fabrics. Some of the blends and fabrics from which it is difficult to remove stains will retain the ink from these markers.

Don't use permanent-ink markers under plastic because the ink bleeds and causes yellowing or blurred lines.

Dried up watercolor markers can be brought back to life by adding water to them. These markers are made of a felt strip impregnated with dye and filled with water. Most of the time they have just dried out, not run out of dye. Fill a disposable syringe, such as diabetics use, with about 10 to 20 CC's of water. Insert the syringe in the small space next to the felt tip and squirt the water into the marker's plastic shell. Place the cap on the marker and shake it up. Leave the marker for about an hour. Try using it. If it is still quite dry, add a tiny bit more water and repeat the process. If the marker is too runny, leave the cap off for a short time to allow it to dry a little. Markers like these can be restored several times before the color is all used up.

Memory Place Mats

Collect pictures, postcards, and newspaper clippings from trips. Use them to make "memory" place mats. Glue them to both sides of a colored tagboard base, cut place mat size. Cover both sides with clear adhesive plastic slightly larger than the place mat. Rub smooth so the plastic adheres well. Go around each glued piece and all around the outside edges of mat. Trim the plastic to a 1/4" border all the way around the mat. This makes it waterproof.

Memory Verses

Use index cards as flash cards for memory verse reviews. Print the verse on one side of the card and the reference on the other side. Flash the reference and have students say the verse. Then reverse the review. Flash the verse and have them give the reference.

Mittens or Hot Mitts

These can be used to make "quickie" bean bags. Decorate them with wiggly eyes, felt, yarn, buttons, markers, etc. Fill them with dried peas, beans, or rice. Don't stuff the mitten too full as it will break open when thrown. Sew it shut securely using several rows of sewing machine stitching or by hand using waxed dental floss.

Music

Make use of students who play musical instruments whenever possible. They can play simple hymns during offering or singing times. Or try using one of the psalms, such as Psalm 150, and have class members add their instruments at appropriate places. This psalm calls for a good variety, such as trumpets (brass or wind instruments), tambourines and cymbals (drums and percussion), and strings (violins, guitars, etc.). Class members who aren't musical can all join in on the "Let everything that breathes praise the Lord."

Overhead Projectors

Use the overhead projector to help you make bulletin board figures. Select a simple pattern, such as one from a clip art book, and make a transparency of it using the copier. If you don't have access to a copier that will make transparencies, trace the figure on the transparency using a marker. Project the picture on a large sheet of paper or poster board. Enlarge it to the desired size and draw it on the paper.

Protect frequently used transparencies by framing them with lightweight cardboard.

Save valuable class time by preparing your lesson on transparencies and using the overhead projector. This method is easier than to write things on the chalkboard.

Paper Clips

Paper clips work well as quickie hangers for classroom use. Unbend them into an "S" shape. Attach the material on one end and hook the other end over nails, pins, nets, etc.

Pictures

Advertisements in magazines frequently have excellent pictures. These are great for your picture file. Just cut off any printing.

Plaster of Paris

To get a smoother plaster, slowly sift the plaster into warm water. Stir this with your hand as you mix it. The mixture should be about like thin pudding.

Play Dough

As a replacement for purchased food dyes for play dough, try using these substitutes:
Red—Boil 3 diced beets in 1 1/2 cups water. Strain.
Pink—Use frozen cranberry juice cocktail, thawed but not diluted.
Yellow—Puree 1/4 cup water and 1 carrot in a blender.
Green—Use a strong brew of alfalfa tea.
Blue—Boil 1 cup of blueberries and 1 cup water for 5 minutes. Strain.
Brown—Dissolve instant cocoa, coffee, or carob in a small amount of water.

Portable Activity Center

Add variety and interest to your teaching by bringing a mystery activity to class each week. Place in a suitcase all the supplies you need for your activity and wheel the suitcase into class on a 2-wheel luggage carrier. Activities could be classroom games, puzzles, puppets, craft projects, object lessons, Bible costumes, reference books, etc.

Poster Board

There is a slight difference between poster board and tagboard. Tagboard is usually cream colored and of a weight that is commonly used for flash cards. Poster board comes in white and many colors and can be found in several different weights.

Posters

When you make a poster publicizing an oft-repeated event, such as roller skating or game night, make it a recyclable poster. Put the visuals and the main information on the poster, but leave a blank space for date, time, and place. You can add this specific information on a separate sheet of paper that can be taped on the poster and removed after the event is over. A variation of this is to cover the poster with clear adhesive plastic and write the specific information in with a marker. The information can be removed and changed at will.

Puzzles

Eliminate the problem of deciding where to put stray puzzle pieces by color coding each puzzle. Put the puzzle together, picture side down. Spray it with a light coat of colored spray paint. Allow to dry and then store. Use a different color for each puzzle. Now when you find a stray piece, simply turn it over and you will know at a glance where it belongs.

Reproducible Materials

Clip and copy art books are great to use as patterns for flannelboard and flannelgraph figures, visualized stories, memory verses, songs, bulletin boards, and finger puppets.

Stickers

You can make your own adhesive stickers for children. Start by drawing geometric shapes, such as squares, circles, or rectangles on a page of typing paper. Drawn your own or use small reproducible pictures that fit into these shapes. Mix equal amounts of Elmer's or Lepage's Mucilage and water together in a small container. Apply this glue mixture to the back of each sticker page with a paintbrush. Let the pages dry completely with the glue side up. Allow children to color the stickers with crayons or watercolor markers. When the pictures are dry, cut out the stickers and dampen the back side of them with a slightly wet sponge or brush.

Styrofoam

Cut Styrofoam with a razor blade, craft knife, or sharp knife that you have run through a bar of soap. To make holes, heat a sharp tool, such as a large needle or nail and poke it through the Styrofoam. Be sure to use pliers or a hot pad when handling the heated tool. Use white glue to connect two pieces of foam together.

Supplies

Use a plastic carry-all, such as the kind used for household cleaning supplies, to store and carry classroom supplies when you are short of storage cabinets. Here is a list of items you might want to include in your classroom supplies:

    pencils
    markers
    scissors
    stapler and staples
    paper clips
    straight pins
    rubber bands
    glue
    transparent tape
    index cards
    chalk
    staple remover
    paper punch
    colored plastic tape
    yarn
    sandpaper
    glue sticks
    tissues

Tape Recorders

When you have a student who is sick, record your class session and give him the cassette along with any handout papers the students received. Classmates can also include greetings or prayers for the sick person. If the homebound student hasn't got a tape recorder, leave one with him so he can play the tape.

Vegetable Oil

You can make drawings or paintings transparent by painting or rubbing vegetable oil on the back of them.

Visuals

Color figures for use on flannelgraphs and bulletin boards with felt-tip markers, crayons, or tempera paint. Color the direction of natural hair or fur. Outline the entire figure with a broad black line for easier visibility. You can use colored paper if the object is mostly one color, such as fruit or animals. For large areas, such as skin, try using lecturer's chalk. These are broad sticks of chalk. Use cotton balls to apply the chalk to the area. Apply plenty of chalk and rub it in smoothly — the smoother the better. Construction paper takes such rubbing well. A clean cotton ball will remove excess chalk. Use the same method and a small amount of pink chalk or cosmetic blush for cheeks. You can also use Cray-Pas as they blend well and are easy to use. Blending can be done with a cotton swab or small piece of paper towel. Color, blend, and rub off excess color. You can use an art eraser to remove "over-the-line" mistakes for both chalk and Cray-Pas.

Yarn

Yarn lengths for sewing or lacing cards will be easier to use if you dip each end into white glue or nail polish and shape it into a point. Allow ends to dry before using.

Here is a list of materials that you can easily collect or recycle into items for classroom use. The directions for making many of these items have been given previously. Check the index for locations. Whenever possible, use recycled materials. This not only cuts down on expenses but is good stewardship of the materials God has entrusted to us.

adding machine tape
adhesive plastic
aluminum foil
aluminum pie pans
aprons
balloons
beads
beans
beeswax
berry boxes
blister packs
boat
books
bottle caps
bottles
branches
bread
brooms
bubble wrap
burlap
butcher paper
buttons
cake pans
calendars
candles
cans
cardboard
cardboard boxes
carpet samples
cereal boxes
chalk
chenille wire
cloth
clothespins
coat hangers
coffee grounds
coloring books

combs
construction paper
cookie cutters
cookie sheets
corks
cornmeal
corrugated cardboard
cotton balls
cotton swabs
craft sticks
crayons
crepe paper
crowns
cup hooks
cutlery trays
dental floss
detergent
dish soap
dishes
doughnut boxes
dowels
drawer liner
drinking straws
egg cartons
embroidery hoops
embroidery patterns
envelopes
fabric dyes
fake fur
feathers
felt
file folders
fishnets
flowers
folding tables
food coloring
freezer paper

frosting mixes
gelatin
gift wraps
glitter
gloves
glue
greeting cards
hot mitts
index cards
Ivory soap
jars
jewelry
jingle bells
keys
label tape
lace
lampshades
leather
lids
light bulbs
magazines
magnets
mailboxes
maps
markers
memo boards
mesh bags
metal rings
milk cartons
mirrors
mittens
monofilament
nails
neckties
newspapers
painter's dropcloth
pans
pantyhose
paper bags
paper clips
paper cups
paper plates
paper towels
paraffin
pasta
peas
pebbles

pellon
phone books
photo albums
photographs
picture frames
pictures
pizza cardboards
plaster of Paris
plastic
plastic bags
plastic bottles
plastic eggs
plastic glass
plastic lids
plastic spoons
plastic tablecloths
plastic tape
polyurethane foam
pom-poms
Popsicle sticks
poster board
pot holders
pots
pudding mixes
pump containers
rhinestones
ribbon rolls
ribbons
rice
rubber bands
rubber stamps
sand
sandpaper
sawdust
seeds
sequins
sewing trims
sheets
shelf paper
shells
shoe bags
shoestrings
shower curtains
silk flowers
socks
spools
starch

stencils	tubes
stickers	tuna cans
Styrofoam sheets	twist metal ties
Styrofoam cartons	vegetable oil
Styrofoam cups	velcro
Styrofoam trays	wallpaper
suction cups	washers
Sunday-school materials	wax paper
tagboard	white glue
tempera paints	wiggle eyes
tissue paper	window shades
tongue depressors	wires
toothbrushes	wooden spoons
toothpicks	yarn
travel brochures	

Because the number of possible items from these and other recycled materials is almost limitless, we have given you directions for a few more in the following pages.

Balloons

Insert student names and addresses for long distance pen pals and have a lift-off for a special occasion.

Use them for review games by inserting memory-verse references or questions. Have students pop them and recite the verses or answer the questions.

Berry Boxes

Use these open weave plastic boxes to create trails of bubbles by dipping them into a soap bubble mixture and waving them in the air.

Weave ribbon or yarn through them to create pretty baskets.

Blister Packs

These are the clear plastic bubbles used so widely in packaging. They make wonderful "glass" frames for craft pictures or small scenes with figurines. Carefully remove the blister from the package and remove excess paper on its surrounding tab. A word of caution—the plastic creases easily and stays creased. Too much handling or trying to wash the plastic may cause it to turn cloudy. Trim the tab to about 1/4" around the blister. Glue the blister to the picture background or scene base and decorate it at the bottom with some sort of trim to cover any paper that might still be visible on the outside tab.

Boat

Even a boat with holes in it is useful. Use it outside as a story center for Bible stories. Many stories have boats in them. Some examples are Noah, Jesus stilling the storm, Jesus calling the disciples, Jesus teaching from a boat, Paul's shipwreck, etc. By taking a class outside to an actual boat and conducting class there, you can add great realism to the stories.

Bottle Caps

You can make a rhythm band tambourine. Punch holes in the caps. Remove the ends from a tin can. Punch holes around the top and bottom rims of the can and wire the caps onto it to form the tambourine. Caps can also be used as playing pieces for games.

Brooms

Use the broom straws for crafts by soaking them in water to soften them. Then press them flat with a hot iron. Glue them onto the surface of old boxes or other bases in geometric patterns. The straws can be dyed different colors for brighter designs. This is a traditional Mexican folk craft.

Bubble Wrap

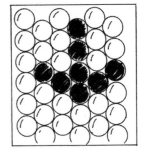

This is the clear plastic protective wrap often used in sending packages. The bubbles can be painted or colored with markers in geometric designs as craft projects.

Cans

Tin cans can be covered with cloth, felt, aluminum foil, tempera paint, or adhesive plastic to make attractive storage containers. By removing both ends of shallow ones like tuna or ham cans, you can make nice foundations for displaying mini figurines. You can also glue them to background bases and use as frames for pictures.

Cardboard

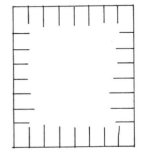

You can make a small hand-weaving loom by taking a piece of cardboard the shape and size of the object you want to make. Make an odd number of 1/2" long slits along the opposite sides of the cardboard on all four sides. Space these slits to allow room for your yarn to fit through them. Tie one end of the yarn to the first notch and lace it back and forth through the notches on the opposite side until the whole piece of cardboard is covered with parallel threads.

Weave over and under these threads with more yarn, working back and forth across the loom. When you have finished weaving all the threads, tie off the yarn. Cut the cardboard away to leave the woven object.

Cardboard Boxes

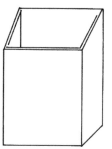

Special storage containers for games kept in 9" x 12" envelopes can be made from laundry detergent boxes. These boxes are sturdy and stand hard use. Cut the box 12" high in back. Then measure down so that the front side measures 9" high. Cut the box so that the sides come down at an angle from the 12" in back to the straight line 9" across in the front. Cover the box with adhesive plastic in a bright, colorful covering. By changing these cuts from the wide front and back to the narrower sides, you can make storage containers for magazines.

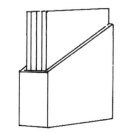

Plastic topped stationery boxes make nice display boxes for fragile items.

Cereal Boxes

Family size boxes make "in/out" boxes for office or classroom. Cut out a side panel and remove the flaps from one end. Cut the sides at an angle for easier reaching.

Clothespins

The clip kind can also be used as stands for small pictures by gluing them to the back sides.

Combs

Two combs with teeth the same size can be used to make a craft loom. Use screws to mount them opposite each other on wooden strips or a frame. String yarn through these teeth and weave through these parallel threads. (See CARDBOARD this section)

Cookie Cutters

These can be used for cutting play dough or maché. They also make nice stencils to draw around.

Cotton Swabs

Make a "pussy willow" picture by drawing a stem on a piece of paper. Break or cut off the swabs and glue them along this stem.

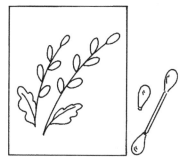

Craft Sticks

Dip them into tempera paint and then drip the paint onto paper to make dip and drip paintings.

Crayons

Use broken and leftover pieces to make crayon figures to delight young students. Remove the outer wrappers and melt the crayons over water. Pour them into candy molds and set them in the freezer section of your refrigerator for about 10-15 minutes. Pop them out and store them as you would regular crayons.

Cutlery Trays

They make good organizers for classroom supplies, such as markers, pencils, pens, erasers, etc.

Dishes

Broken ceramic dishes make nice mosaic tiles for craft projects.

Egg Cartons

Turn a carton upside down and use it as an organizer by sticking scissors, pencils, etc. into the cups.

Cut sections of colored Styrofoam cartons apart to make flowers. Cut petals in each section and glue a small pom-pom, button, or bead in the center.

Use Styrofoam ones for paints. Give each student a 4-egg section with a different color of paint in each section.

It can become a review box. Cut a slit in the top of each section. Write review questions on slips of paper. Fold these up and slip one into each section. Leave part of the slip sticking out the slit. Students draw out a slip and answer the question. This can be done as an individual or team review.

Make rhythm band bells by tying a jingle bell in an individual carton section. The ends of the yarn used to fasten the bell in the section make a good handle.

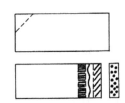

Envelopes

letter size
Cut off envelope corners for bookmarks.

For fun costume bracelets, seal an envelope and mark it into narrow bands. Decorate these bands with crayons or markers. Cut them apart.

You can make a whole town and scenery out of envelopes. Seal the envelope. At both sides of one end, cut a 1 1/2" slit. Turn the resulting flaps upward and glue them to about a 3" tag- or poster-board square. Trim the envelope to a desired shape and add details to the building with markers or crayons. Trees are made by using a 2" center as the trunk and drawing the desired top branches from the rest of the envelope. Glue these trees to smaller pieces of tag-board or poster board.

Felt

Cut scraps of felt into geometric shapes and let students arrange them on the flannelboard for art projects or to tell a story.

Glue

When white glue becomes too dried out to use normally, make play dough out of it. Mix equal amounts of glue, flour, and corn-starch together until well blended. You can keep the consistency controlled easily by adding a few drops of glue if it is too dry or flour and cornstarch if it is too wet. Various colors can be made by adding food colors to the glue before you mix it with the flour and cornstarch. This glue-dough can be kept in a tightly closed plastic bag for several weeks. It will harden without baking. Make holes for beads or hanging items by placing a toothpick or plastic drinking straw in the item and removing this when dry.

Greeting Cards

The fronts can be cut off to make memory verse reminders, invitations, puzzles, or mobiles.

You can also cut the fronts into different shapes and lace them together with yarn for baskets.

Jars

Small glass jars, such as from baby food, make nice snow scenes. Glue a plastic figure inside the cap with waterproof glue. Fill the jar with water and 1/4 tsp moth crystals or glitter. Seal the jar lid shut with waterproof glue. Shake the jar up to make it "snow."

Keys

These can be used as clappers in glass bottles or tin cans to make wind chimes.

Lampshades

A restored lampshade can become a handy bulletin board for a classroom short of display space. Cover the shade with cloth, felt, wallpaper, patterned adhesive plastic or spray paint it. Hang it from the ceiling or a pipe or mount it on a wooden stand. Memory verses, pictures, prayer reminders, etc. can be pinned or taped to the shade just as to a bulletin board. If desired, you can also hang objects from the bottom using yarn or monofilament.

Lids

Lids from juice cans or glass jars make good foundation frames for mini pictures or ornaments. Cut the picture to fit in the lid and glue it in place. Trim the outside with ribbon or braid. Use a ribbon or yarn loop for hanging.

Lids can also be used as jumbo message buttons. Paint or glue your message to the rounded side of the lid. Cut a cardboard circle the same size as the concave side of the lid. Tape a safety pin to this circle. Insert the cardboard in the lid and glue it in place.

Light Bulbs

Make Christmas ornaments by dipping burned-out bulbs into paint. Trim them with glitter, ribbon, sequins, etc. Wrap fine wire around the screw part to form a hanger.

Light bulbs can also be used for maracas for a rhythm band. Cover the bulb with a 1/4" thick layer of papier mache. Allow this to dry thoroughly. Tap the mache' form on a flat surface until the bulb inside it breaks and the glass rattles. Paint and decorate the maracas as desired.

Magazines

Craft beads can be made from brightly colored pages by cutting them into small triangles or rectangles. Coat one side of these pieces with white glue. Wrap it around a toothpick or hairpin to form a bead. Glue the outer flap down tightly. Let the bead dry, r move it from the toothpick and string it on yarn or monofilamen

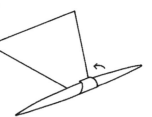

Markers

When the marker itself can't be restored anymore for drawing, cut the plastic tube into short pieces and use them for beads.

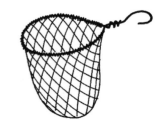

Mesh Bags

Turn these into insect nets for nature walks. Bend clothes hanger

wire into a circle the same size as the opening of the bag. Attach the bag to it with overstitching. A handle can be made out of the wire that is left over.

Milk Cartons

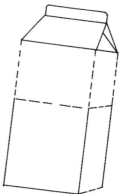

These make good play blocks. Cut the pointed top off. Slit each corner down about 5 inches and fold the resulting flaps inside. Tape shut. The blocks can be covered with adhesive plastic or decorated with permanent-ink markers if desired.

Cartons also make nice planters because they are waterproof. Cut them off at the desired length and decorate as desired.

Mirrors

Use broken pieces and combine them with broken dish fragments to create a pretty craft mosaic. Because of the danger of cutting fingers, this is a project for older students or best done wearing rubber gloves.

Nails

You can make a simple rhythm band instrument by simply banging two large nails together.

By hanging several large nails on a clothes hanger frame with monofilament, you can create a windchime.

Neckties

Out-of-style neckties make good storage containers for pencils, crayons, and markers. Starting at the wide tip, cut the tie off about 4" longer than the items to be stored in it. Turn it inside out and seam it to close the bottom of the cut. Sew half a snap or velcro piece on the wide tip and the matching piece on the tie to form a fold-over top.

Ties also can be used as belts or headbands for Bible costumes.

Painter's Drop Cloth

This or other plastic sheeting can be cut into transparencies for overhead projectors.

Paper Bags

Make lumienaria lanterns by folding bag tops down several times. Add about 3-4" of sand in the bottom. Stick a candle remnant in this sand and light the candle. This is a traditional Christmas decoration around houses in Latin America and Mexico.

You can also make a review grab bag by placing questions or memory verse references in the bag. Students draw them out and answer the question or say the verse.

Paper Plates

Plaques with pockets for holding notepads, pencils, etc. can be made by using two regular paper plates. Cut one plate in half. Invert this half over the inside surface of the first plate and glue it in place.

Phone Books

These make great places to press flowers and leaves for craft projects.

Photo Albums

Cut the pages into sections and recycle these to make flip books. (See FLIP BOOKS in the index for directions.)

Photographs

Use these for visuals. See section below for further details.

Pictures

Pictures can be used to make visualized songs and memory verses, "mix and match the pictures" book or games, stick and finger puppets, bulletin boards, flannelgraphs, flash card stories, stand-up figures, figures for pocket charts or Styrofoam boards, games, puzzles.

Use pictures also for teaching pictures. Collect cartoons and cut off the captions. Use the picture parts for discussion. Use close-up faces, and students can practice witnessing to them as a warm-up for real people.

Picture Frames

Make craft looms by removing the glass and hammering small nails evenly on two opposite sides of the frame. Use yarn for weaving, following directions on cardboard looms previously mentioned.

Plastic Bottles

clear bottles

Use these for "glass" domes to protect figures. For the latter, cut a pop bottle off about 3" from the top. Then remove the neck by using a heated knife to melt the plastic. Cut a cardboard circle the size of the bottom of your "dome" to become the base of your display. Glue figurines, artificial flowers, etc. to this to make a mini scene. Glue the plastic dome to this base. Cut another cardboard circle large enough to cover the hole in the top of the plastic dome. Cover this circle with felt or cloth as desired and glue it in place over the top hole. Trim the outside edges of top and bottom circles with braid or ric-rac if desired. You can also substitute a plastic glass for the bottle if you prefer.

colored bottles

Craft pinwheels are easy to make. Cut a square from a side of the bottle. Make slits in all four corners of the square. Fold every other point in to the center and fasten them with a small nail to a dowel. Leave the nail loose enough to allow the pinwheel to spin easily.

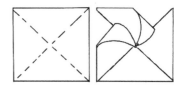

Make a craft supply caddy for crayons, scissors, markers, etc. Cut out the sections on each side of upper third of the bottle leaving the neck and two handle strips.

Plastic Lids

Use these as bases for mobiles and hang pieces around the rims.

They also make good craft stencils. Cut the desired design in the flat bottom with a razor blade or craft knife. These stencils can be pinned to paper or material or taped on a wood surface.

You can also fasten jingle bells around the rim of a lid and use it for a tambourine for a rhythm band.

Plastic Tablebloths

Clear tablecloths can act as a protective cover to display items on your classroom tabletop. Tape the items to the table so they don't slip away. This is a good way to review lessons.

Pump Containers

They make great containers for craft mixtures, such as cold water dyes or paints. Spray the mixture on cloth or paper laid over newspaper to get unusual spatter effects.

Ribbon Rolls

Use the plastic kind used for gift wrap ribbon to make frames for craft ornaments or mobiles. Glue a picture to the back of the roll. Glue ribbon or yarn around the roll, leaving enough for a hanger on top.

Seeds

These make good ingredients for mosaics or collages, crafts, add-a-feel pictures, and bean bags.

You can also use them as craft beads. Wash them, and while they are still wet and soft, string them with a large needle and thread on waxed dental floss. Let seeds dry thoroughly.

Sheets

Recycle these for costumes. They also make good banners. Cut a piece to desired size and decorate it with permanent-ink markers or fabric dyes.

Shelf Paper

Use a roll of shelf paper for murals, graffiti projects, collages, etc.

Shells

Like seeds, they are good ingredients for collages, add-a-feel pictures, and banners.

Use them also for wind chimes. Drill a hole in each shell for hanging. String the shells with yarn, monofilament, or string and hang them from a plastic lid or wire clothes hanger base.

Shoe Bags

These have good organizer pockets for classroom supplies, such as markers, glue sticks, scissors, etc.

Shower Curtains

Cut a full-length craft apron using a cobbler style pattern. Attach yarn, cloth, or necktie strips for ties.

Socks

Slip a pair of wooly socks over your jeans and shoes and take your students on an autumn nature walk. Seeds and weeds will stick to the socks, and you can study them back in the classroom.

Spools

These make good beads for small children. Use shoelaces or yarn for stringing the spools.

Use large spools for pretty ornaments. Paint the top and bottom

of the spool or glue a bright circle of felt to them. Glue a piece of ribbon around the spool. Use a piece of metallic thread or monofilament to thread a ribbon bow or large bead through the bottom of the spool to the top and another bead at the top. Leave a length of the cord or monofilament at the top to hang the ornament.

Styrofoam Trays

Use these trays for stencils (see plastic lids) or "rubber" stamps. They can also be used like balsa wood in craft projects. Use them as frame bases to glue pictures in.

Tuna Cans

These can make "mini pans" for melting crayons or wax for craft projects. Add a wire coat hanger handle by wrapping the wire around the can.

Twist Metal Ties

Use ties as "instant" hangers for lightweight objects, like pictures or memory verses, by bending the tie into an S shape. They can also be used as joining rings for flash-card stories or songs.

Wallpaper

Samples or leftovers can be used for bulletin board borders and letters. Wallpaper can also be cut and rolled for beads (see magazines). Another use is for puppet stage backgrounds.

Washers

Flat hardware washers can be sewn on clothes for trims or used on banners to add a unique touch.

Yarn

Create pictures by cutting yarn into pieces and gluing the pieces on a background paper to make designs.

Index

95